CAMBRIDGESHIRE
LIBRARIES
WITHDRAWN
FROM STOCK

*Reminiscences
of Fen and Mere*

REMINISCENCES OF FEN AND MERE

J. M. HEATHCOTE

A new edition with an Introduction by
EDWARD STOREY

OLD SOKE BOOKS
PETERBOROUGH
1994

© Introduction, Edward Storey, 1994

Published by

OLD SOKE BOOKS
68 Burghley Road
Peterborough
PE1 2QE

Thanks from the publisher to
PHILIP HARBURN
for the loan of the original copy

New material typeset by Paul Watkins (Publishing), Stamford
Printed by Woolnough Bookbinding, Irthlingborough

INTRODUCTION

First of all, let me say how delighted I am that this book by J. M. Heathcote is going to be in print again for the first time since it was published in 1876.

It was not the first book to be written on the subject and its author readily acknowledges his debt to others who have ploughed the same furrow, particularly Sir William Dugdale, whose *History of Imbanking and Drayning the Fens* (published in the seventeenth century) provided the foundation for much of the writing which was to follow. Thomas Macauley's *History of England* had also been published in 1855 and included a large section on the Fens, up to the end of the previous century. Another writer who cannot be overlooked is Charles Kingsley who, in both *Hereward the Wake* (1866) and his *Prose Idylls* (1873) gave some of the best descriptions of the Fens that can be found anywhere. Take, for instance, this extract from his novel on Hereward:

> Overhead the arch of heaven spread more ample than elsewhere, as over the open sea; and that vastness gave, and still gives, such cloudlands, such sunrises, such sunsets, as can be seen nowhere else within these isles ... (But) dark and sad were those short autumn days, when all the distances were shut off and the air choked with foul brown fog and drenching rains from all the eastern sea; and pleasant the bursting forth of the keen north-east wind with all its whirling snowstorms. For though it sent men hurrying out into the storm to drive the cattle in from the fen and lift the sheep out of the

snow-wreaths, yet all knew that after the snow would come the keen frost and bright sun and cloudless blue sky, and the fenman's holiday when, work being impossible, all gave themselves up to play and swarmed upon the ice on skates and sledges, to run races, township against township ... Such was the Fenland – hard, yet cheerful, rearing a race of hard and cheerful men, showing their power in old times in valiant fighting ...

There we have both a description of the changing landscape and an assessment of the men who lived in the Fens nearly nine hundred years ago. Similarly, in his *Prose Idylls,* Kingsley is equally convincing:

It was a hard place to live in, the old Fen; a place wherein one heard of 'unexampled instances of longevity', for the same reason that one hears of them in savage tribes – that few lived to old age at all, save those iron constitutions which nothing could break down ... To describe how the Fen came to be one must go back, it seems to me, to an age before all history; an age which cannot be measured by years or centuries; an age shrouded in mystery and to be spoken of only in guesses... No one has ever seen a fen-bank break, without honouring the stern quiet temper which there is in these men, when the north-easter is howling above, the spring tide roaring outside, the brimming tide-way lapping up to the dyke-top, or flying over in sheets of spray; when round the one fatal thread which is trickling over the dyke – or worse, through some forgotten rat's hole in its side, hundreds of men are clustered, without tumult, without complaint, marshalled under their employers, fighting the brute powers of nature ...

One thing in common with most writers on the Fens is their awareness that there has always been – always will be – this constant battle between Man and Nature. It is because of this annual conflict, generation after generation, that the Fens have bred that 'race of hard and cheerful men', stubborn, proud, resilient and wary.

INTRODUCTION

Another writer not usually associated with the Fens is Hilaire Belloc, who was only six years old when Heathcote first published his *Reminiscences of Fen and Mere*. Belloc had also read Dugdale and later came to see the Fens for himself. In 1906, when he published his collection of essays *Hills and the Sea*, it contained three chapters about the Fen-country and its families. Again he provides an excellent introduction to the area by describing how this part of England came into existence and what one should do to understand it:

> Upon the very limit of the Fens, not a hundred feet in height, but very sharp against the level, there is a lonely little hill. From the edge of that hill the land seems very vague; the flat line of the horizon is the only boundary, and that horizon mixes into watery clouds. No countryside is so formless until one has seen the plan of it set down in a map, but on studying such a map one understands the scheme of the Fens.
>
> The Wash is in the shape of a keystone with the narrow side towards the sea and the broad side towards the land. Imagine the Wash prolonged for twenty or thirty miles inland and broadened considerably as it proceeded as would a curving fan, or better still, a horseshoe, and you have the Fens; a horse-shoe whose points, as Dugdale says, are the corners of Lincolnshire and Norfolk... Great catastrophes have certainly overcome this countryside. The greatest was the anarchy of the sixteenth century; but it is probable that, coincidentally with every grave lesion in the continuity of our civilization, the Fens suffered, for they always needed the perpetual attention of man to keep them fully inhabited and cultured.
>
> Nowhere that I have been to in the world does the land fade into the sea so inconspicuously.

Like Kingsley, Belloc felt it necessary to relate the nature of the land to the nature of the people. It was an area he was drawn to because of its mystery and its uniqueness.

REMINISCENCES OF FEN AND MERE

Since then we have had several volumes from H. C. Darby, including *The Drainage of the Fens* (1940); *The Medieval Fenland* (1940) and *The Changing Fenland* (1983); we have also had historical studies from J. Wentworth Day, Alan Bloom, A. K. Astbury and Dorothy Summers, and the personal writings of Sybil Marshall – all adding to our knowledge of the area. Twentieth-century novelists, too, have found that this undramatic landscape is worth exploring and using for their dramas. The first was probably Dorothy L. Sayers in *The Nine Tailors* (1934), followed by L. P. Hartley in *The Brickfield* (1964) and, more recently, Graham Swift's *Waterland* (1983).

Both Dorothy L. Sayers and L. P. Hartley had spent much of their childhood in the Fens and knew the countryside intimately. As Hartley wrote in *The Brickfield*:

> Driving in the Fens was a more dangerous experience than driving in other parts of the country, for every road, or nearly every road, was bordered by a dyke – one of the myriad waterways that drain the Fens... There was no more movement in the water than there were gradients on the road; the only hills the fenmen knew were the artificial slopes that led to bridges. Between the road and its attendant dykes the grass verges often narrowed, leaving little room for error on the driver's part... My life was confined by prohibitions and inhibitions, like the water in a Fen Drain...

The reason for quoting so liberally from these other writers is, I'm sure, clear. The Fens have not been without their own traditions or legends, nor have they been as devoid of literature as we are sometimes led to believe. Accused, as they so often are, of being flat, dull, characterless, bleak and uninteresting, they have, nevertheless, still appealed to many people – historians, poets, novelists, artists and composers, and will continue to do so for they offer us a country within a country, a 'world by itself' and are constantly worthy of study,

INTRODUCTION

especially as we are living in a time of even greater change than those writers I have mentioned.

So, you might ask, what makes this publication different from all the others, and why bother to re-print it? I like it because it is a personal, unpretentious work that mixes history with anecdote, fact with autobiography, statistics with supposition and is full of enthusiasm for its subject. It is like receiving a letter from a friend – 'I was in London when the news arrived that Marshland Sluice was in ruins.'

Heathcote is particularly at ease when writing of the Fens in winter, and especially fen-skating:

> The ice was good. The scenery of the Fen rivers, at all times beautiful in the eyes of those who appreciate Dutch art, is peculiarly so in the winter. The mills, of varied form and colour, are conspicuously placed on the banks; cottages also, such as modern thought has learned to despise and calumniate, with willow and trees denuded of leaves, make most picturesque groups...

> While on the subject of skating, let us suppose that we have put on our pattens prepared to enjoy the fresh, breezy air and the genial sun of a fine winter's morning on Whittlesea Mere. We pass up one of the lodes and find a wide expanse of frozen water. The ice upon the Mere varied much from year to year and often took a different phase during the same frost. There was the hard, black, smooth ice, which, by a little skimming of snow with slight thaw and subsequent frost, would be made white... There was also the anchor ice, so called when it froze under the surface and on it at the same cold temperature... There was the bright ice, which when hard and slippery was called 'glib'. The cracking of the ice was a curious incident, making a loud noise which was heard a long distance at night. We will now imagine the ice to be perfect and that there is a great gathering for a race. About the intended place of starting a good crowd is collected. There is an old

REMINISCENCES OF FEN AND MERE

woman sitting 'with chestnuts in her lap' and roasting others in an old grate. A Dutch oven is by her side and a crowd of buyers round her close by ...

Were I to continue with that extract it would spoil your own enjoyment of it later on in the book, but I hope it illustrates how J. M. Heathcote skilfully lures his reader into the scene, imparting information with his poetic descriptions. Indeed, there is much to learn from these pages for although the author has 'participated in its amusements associated with its inhabitants, and watched the great strides of improvement which have been made during the present century' this is an erudite addition to fenland literature.

We are taken through all the stages of the Fens' development, from their prehistoric beginnings up to the conditions that prevailed at the time of this book being written. As Heathcote said in his own Introduction:

> I am desirous of casting a retrospective glance over the former history of the Fens and of recalling a few reminiscences of those objects and that scenery which are rapidly passing away.

His subjects range from fossil remains to turf-cutting, from the establishment of the religious settlements in the Fens to the drainage of Whittlesea Mere and the storage of water. There are moments when he appears remarkably modern and topical:

> In whatever direction we look for the further improvement of the Fens, the supply of fresh water will become more and more an object of consideration, as an indispensable necessity for meeting the requirements of modern life and for satisfying the demands of recent legislation.

That reads more like an article on conservation written in 1994 than an opinion expressed in 1876.

In conclusion I can do no better than quote from the author's own chapter entitled *Conclusion*:

INTRODUCTION

I have now gone through my recollections of past times as regards this Fen country... Though the Fens are not generally regarded with much favour, or thought a desirable country to live in, I am attached to them from early associations and long residence. The inhabitants of low countries, as a matter of history, have a deep attachment to their own locality.

Anyone associated with the Fens, in whatever capacity, will be enriched by this man's love affair with his 'locality' and we should be grateful that these *Reminiscences* are available again, complete with the sketches the author made at the time of writing. They may not be great works of art but they still manage to evoke something of the Fens' isolation and magical qualities.

This book will delight those of us who do not need convincing and will, I trust, win many converts from those who still need persuading that these spacious fens are, in the words of Charles Kingsley 'beautiful, after their kind.'

Edward Storey
Peterborough 1994

FEN AND MERE

'Hier ein friedfertiges Fischer- und Hirtenvolk, in einem vergessenen Winkel Europens, den es noch mühsam der Meeresfluth abgewann; die See sein Gewerbe, sein Reichthum und seine Plage, eine freie Armuth sein höchstes Gut, sein Ruhm, seine Tugend'—SCHILLER

A pastoral people, inhabiting a neglected corner of Europe, which by industry they have won from the waters of the ocean; the sea their profession, the source of their wealth and their disquietude; their highest good, their glory, and their virtue have all sprung from poverty and freedom

DESERTED MILL IN WINTER.

BY E.W. COOKE R.A.

"WHITTLESEA MERE, FROM THE ROUNDHILL" 1829.

BY P. DEWINT.

REMINISCENCES

of

FEN AND MERE

BY

J. M. HEATHCOTE

LONDON
LONGMANS, GREEN, AND CO.
1876

All rights reserved

LONDON: PRINTED BY
SPOTTISWOODE AND CO., NEW-STREET SQUARE
AND PARLIAMENT STREET

DEDICATED
TO
EDWARD FELLOWES, Esq., M.P.

RAMSEY ABBEY.

I have purposely abstained from mentioning the name of any of those who have laboured so ably and so well in promoting the improvement of the Fen Country; but I dedicate my little volume to the present Chairman of the Middle Level Commissioners, because I wish to take the opportunity of expressing my esteem for an old friend, and my high appreciation of that constant and unremitting attention which, during so many years, he has paid to the general business of the Fens, and of the ability which he has shown in discharging the various duties of his important office.

INTRODUCTION.

HAVING spent a long life in the immediate neighbourhood of the Fens; having participated in its amusements, associated with its inhabitants, and watched the great strides of improvement which have been made during the present century; having, moreover, taken a humble part in the transaction of that business and the promotion of those measures by which the more recent progress has been effected, I am desirous of casting a retrospective glance over the former history of the Fens, and of recalling a few reminiscences of those objects and that scenery which are rapidly passing away, and which seem likely to be soon totally forgotten. I hope that even a cursory record of facts may serve to revive an interest in by-gone days, and may even now form an attractive page in the History of British Industry. I propose more especially to address those who wish to recall to memory the annals of their own district, and my object will be to show the progress and improvement which have there taken place. I have availed myself freely of authentic sources, while, in addition to my own observations, I have made use of information which has been communicated to me by some of the oldest inhabitants. Among the works of which I have occasionally availed myself are Dugdale's 'History of the Fen,' the well-known little work entitled 'The Camp of Refuge,' and various papers contributed to periodicals by the Rev. E. Bradley. My quotations are sometimes abridged, and I have not felt it necessary in all cases to indicate them by inverted commas. These materials I have endeavoured to arrange in some sort of chronological order; and the general effect of the narrative will, I hope, be to excite feelings of thankfulness and hope in the hearts of Fenmen. The history of our country during the last 500 or 600 years has been eminently the history of moral, physical, and intellectual progress; and no one who is correctly informed of the past will be disposed to take a desponding view of the future. We shall unquestionably have to notice many retrograde steps, many contests maintained by prejudice and error, large sums wasted in opposition to the onward march of events, frequent failures of large and important measures. But the acknowledged fact that within the space of thirty-five years the annual rental of 250,000 acres, forming one-third of the area comprised in the Bedford Level, has increased 100 per cent. affords a valuable lesson to the present and coming generation, and bears testimony to the same qualities of mind and the same perseverance under difficulties, and gives promise of the same ultimate success in overcoming them, which have ever distinguished the inhabitants of a Low Country.

J. M. HEATHCOTE.

January, 1876.

CONTENTS.

PART I.

CHAPTER   PAGE

I. General condition of the Fens, and the way in which they were silted up 1

II. Fossil remains—Letter from Professor Sedgwick . 3

III. State of the country and its inhabitants—Extracts from the 'Camp of Refuge;' from Dugdale's 'History of the Fen;' Popular Ballad against improvement of the Fen; Extracts from Macaulay's 'History of England,' and from Arthur Young . 5

IV. Crowland Abbey, Camden's Account . . 15

V. St. Gurlach's Visit to Crowland . . . 17

VI. Anecdotes current in the last century—Revellers . 19

PART II.

I. Notices of Whittlesea Mere 26

II. Connington and Ramsey 27

III. Ramsey Abbey 30

IV. The *Bure* and Setting Trimmers . . . 33

CHAPTER		PAGE
V.	Fen Scenery and Artists—Letter from E. W. Cooke, R.A.—Mirage—Letter from Professor Sedgwick	35
VI.	Facts relating to lands adjoining Whittlesea Mere	41
VII.	The Old Fen Mill	44
VIII.	Snipe-shooting - The Plover—The Decoy	46
IX.	The Fen in time of Frost	50
X.	A Stalking-sledge	55
XI.	Birds—Flowers—Insects	58
XII.	Cutting Turf	62
XIII.	Value and Produce of Land	64

PART III.

I.	Various schemes of Drainage	67
II.	Drainage of Whittlesea Mere	69
III.	Appold's Pump	76
IV.	The Strata below the Mere—The 'Nut' deposit—Opinion of Sir William Hooker	79
V.	Relics found below the Mere	85
VI.	Early cultivation of the bed of the Mere	88
VII.	Breaking of Marshland Sluice—Siphons	94
VIII.	Inundations	97
IX.	The North Level	98
X.	The New Dock at Lynn	100
XI.	Parliamentary Taxes in the three Levels	101
XII.	Conclusion of Part III.	103

PART IV.

CHAPTER	PAG
I. Future of the Fens	105
II. Storage of Water	109
III. Future Cultivation—The Estuary	111
IV. Conclusion	113

APPENDIX.

ENGLISH FEN AND IRISH BOG.

SECTION	
I. Character of the Irish Bog Country and its Inhabitants	118
II. Buried Remains and Fossils	119
III. Origin and Formation of Irish Bog	122
IV. Moving Bogs	126
V. Extent of Irish Bog—Prospects of Drainage and Reclamation	128
VI. Utilization of Peat	130
Letter by S. B. J. Skertchly, F.G.S.	132
Conclusion	133

ILLUSTRATIONS.

'Deserted Mill in Winter,' *by E. W. Cooke, R.A.*   *Frontispiece*
'Whittlesea Mere from the Round Hill, 1829,'
    by P. Dewint . . . . *To face Frontispiece*
Peterborough Cathedral . . . . *to face p.* 8
Ely Cathedral . . . . . ,, 12
Crowland Abbey . . . . . ,, 15
Crowland Bridge . . . . . ,, 16
Connington Castle, 1800 . . . . ,, 27
Connington Castle, 1875 . . . . ,, 28
Boat-gate of Whittlesea Mere and the *Bure* . ,, 33
Regatta on Whittlesea Mere, 1842 . . . ,, 39
Mills used for Draining the Fens . . . ,, 44
Mill with Skaters drawing a Sledge . . . ,, 51
Skaters on Fen Drain . . . . ,, 52
Skating on Whittlesea Mere, 1835–6 . . ,, 52
Skaters and Sledges . . . . ,, 53
Old Woman selling Chestnuts . . . ,, 53
Groups on the Ice . . . . . ,, 54
Race on Whittlesea Mere . . . . ,, 54
Reed Harvest . . . . . ,, 55
Cutting Reed . . . . . ,, 55

Cutting Sedge	*to face p.* 55
Stacking Reed	,, 55
Stalking Sledge	,, 56
Loading Turf at Story's Bridge . . .	,, 63
Post or Gauge, showing the Depression of Soil since the Drainage of Whittlesea Mere . .	,, 89
Inundation of 1862	,, 94
Thorney Abbey	,, 99

MAPS.

Map of Fens, 1723	,, 1
Map of Fens, 1875	,, 1
Map of Whittlesea Mere	,, 26

MAP OF FENS, 1723.

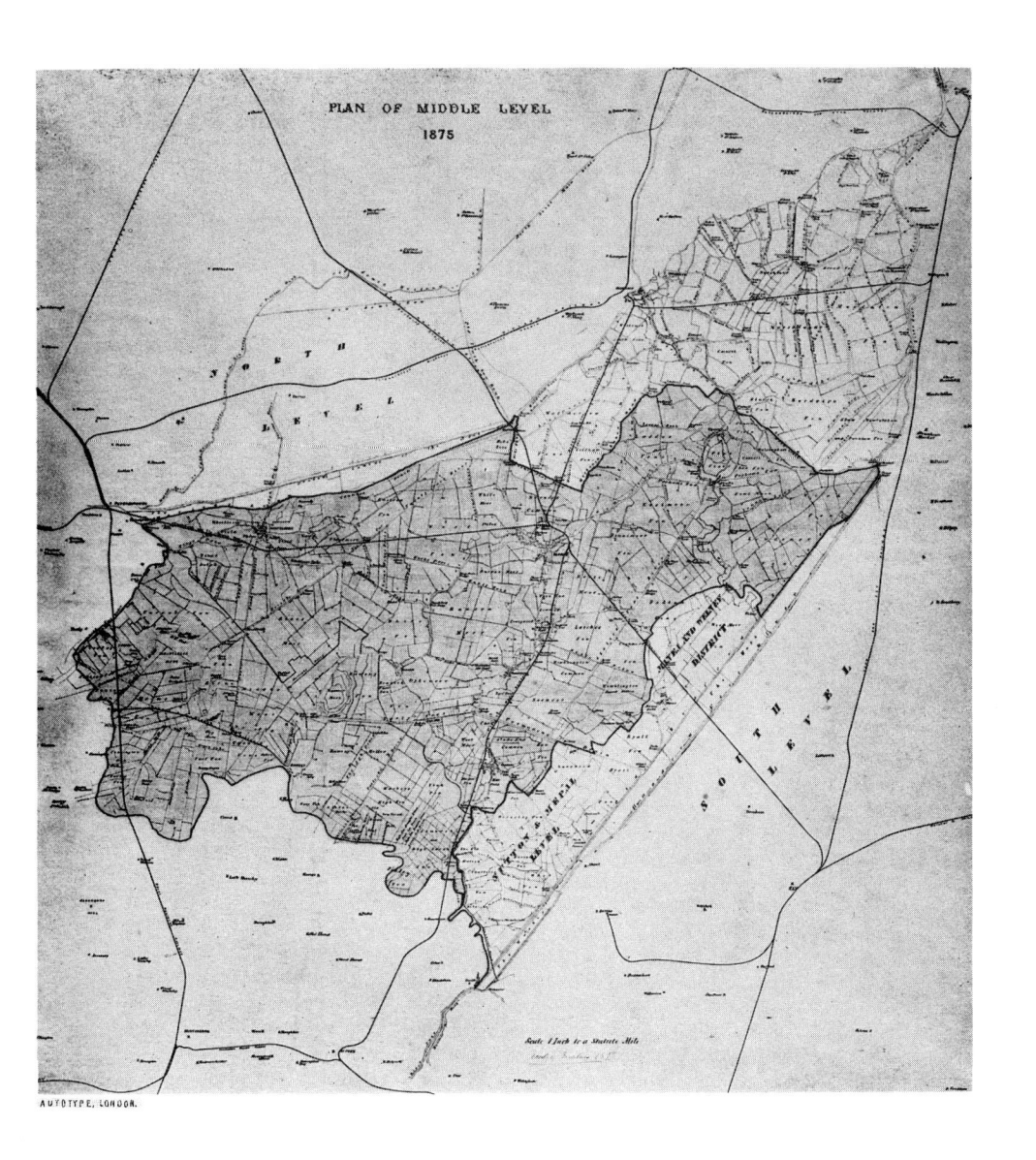

MAP OF FENS, 1875.

Errata.

P. 2, line 19, *for* Skirbeach *read* Skyrbeck
,, 9 ,, 24, *omit* from Armstrong's 'History of Lynn,' *read* as the 'Powtes Complaint'
,, 14 ,, 3, *for* Seam *read* Leam
,, 17, lines 7 and 16, *for* Gurlach *read* Guthlake
,, 18, line 1, *for* Gurlach *read* Guthlake
,, 37 ,, 27, for *Nuphai* read *Nuphar*
,, 54 ,, 5, *for* Gittan *read* Gittam
,, 59 ,, 20, for *Marsus Ranæ (hydrocharis)* read *Hydrocharis morsus ranæ*
,, 59 ,, 22 ,, *globutifera* read *globulifera*
,, 60 ,, 9 ,, *Bottomia* read *Hottonia*
,, 60 ,, 10 ,, *Nymphœa lutea* and *alba* read *Nymphœa alba* and *Nuphar lutea*
,, 60 ,, 13 ,, *Achilles Pharmici* read *Achillea ptarmica*
,, 60 ,, 25 ,, *Stirpus* read *Scirpus*
,, 86 ,, 8, *for* 40 *read* 10 or 12
,, 87 ,, 8, for *N*. read *Nuphar*
,, 89 ,, 13, *for* is now *read* was then
,, 93, lines 25 and 26, *for* on each acre was grown 20 tons *read* on these 3 acres were grown 20 tons
,, 99, line 19, *for* 175,888 acres *read* 175·88 acres
,, 102 ,, 17 ,, 600,000 *read* 60,000
,, 106 ,, 1 ,, sluice *read* cut

Errata.

Page 48, line 12 *for* covey *read* coccy.
,, 81, ,, 3 ,, stool ,, stools.
,, 96, ,, 22 ,, 4 inches ,, 4 feet.

REMINISCENCES OF FEN AND MERE.

PART I.

CHAPTER I.

THE GENERAL CONDITION OF THE FENS, AND HOW THEY BECAME SILTED UP.

A REFERENCE to the Maps which are prefixed will show the geographical position of the FENS. It will be seen that the district is bounded 'on all parts by highlands, in the form of a horse-shoe, which makes it like a bay, from that point of land about Hunstanton in Norfolk to Wynthorpe in Lincolnshire.'

<small>Dugdale, History of the Fen, c. 33, p. 172.</small>

The general condition of all parts of the low country, the various strata which underlie the surface, and the objects which are discovered in them, sufficiently prove that during the lapse of ages great changes in the surface have taken place, that the level has materially altered, that forest-trees once grew there luxuriantly, and that the climate, the flora, and the animals are entirely different from what they once were. 'Great numbers of trees have been dug up, such as oak and fir, which will not live in water. When the Wisbeach river was deepened, the workmen found, eight feet below the then bottom, which was stony, several boats within short distances of each other, which had been overwhelmed by the silt for many ages. So likewise at Salter's Lode, at the digging of the foundation of the fosse, the silt was found to be ten feet deep, and next below it, three feet of fen moor, then bluish gault with the roots of trees in it; next, moor three feet thick, firmer and cleaner than the other; and lastly, whitish clay. Likewise, of late years, at Whittlesea Mere, when digging through the moor, at eight feet deep, they came to a perfect soil and swaths of grass, lying as they were first mown down. At Skirbeach sluice, near Boston, there was found, at sixteen feet deep, covered with silt, a smith's forge and all the tools thereunto belonging, horse-shoes and other things made of iron. In erecting a sluice in Marshland, about a mile to the west of Magdalen Bridge, at a depth of seventeen feet, were found furze-bushes and trees standing in solid earth below the silt; several species of them lie embedded in peat and resting on clay.

'From the foregoing facts Dugdale draws the conclusion that this vast level was once a firm and dry land, and not annoyed with any extraordinary inundation from the sea, or stagnation of fresh waters; that some great land-flood, many ages since, meeting an obstruction at the natural ostiaries towards the sea, by reason of much silt, which, after a long drought, had choked them up, did then spread itself over the whole level, and the waters ever since covering the same have produced a moor, now grown to this thickness.

CHAPTER II.

FOSSILS.

I HAD some conversation in 1864 with Professor Sedgwick on the subject of the fossils which had been discovered in the Fen. He showed me some dug up long ago at March, Littleport, and Ely; and for further particulars he referred me to his assistant, Mr. Seeley, of Sidney College. The following are a list of specimens which I saw in his collection :—The teeth and tail-bone of a hippopotamus, vertebræ and teeth of a rhinoceros, horns of a goat similar to the ibex, wing and breast-bone of wild and tame swan, *Bos primigenius* from Stretham, in the Isle of Ely; elephant; *Bos longifrons*; head and teeth of *Canis lupus* or wolf; *Cervus capreolus* or small deer; *Castor Europæus* or beaver; otter, roebuck, and red deer; the elk (Irish *Cervus Megaceros*), walrus, and horse. In the gravel were found marine shells (*Tellina solidula Astarte*) characteristic of the Arctic regions; the *Turritella communis* from March; several beds of *Linnæa paludina*. The fossil bones of a large animal were taken up in the bed of Whittlesea Mere and shown to Professor Owen, who pronounced them to be those of the grampus. The skeleton, in a very perfect state, is now in the possession of J. Laurance, Esq., of Elton. This fact I communicated to Professor Sedgwick, who returned me the following answer, which may have sufficient interest to justify my giving it verbatim :

'March 6, 1865.

'My dear Sir,—I am not surprised that remains of the grampus have been found in the neighbouring Fens, but I am surprised to hear that a skeleton of that genus was discovered when Whittlesea Mere was laid dry. Was the skeleton in the alluvial silt at the bottom of the old lake? or was it dug out of the stratum on which the lake rested? The existence of a skeleton such as you mention seems to indicate that, in consequence of a change of level, the sea sent a shallow estuary up as far as the Mere, and that the grampus, in chase of its food, had run up too far, and been stranded. I have a portion of a whale's vertebræ, but I do not know under what conditions it was found.

'Yours ever,
'ADAM SEDGWICK.'

CHAPTER III.

STATE OF THE COUNTRY AND ITS INHABITANTS.

A LITTLE work entitled the 'Camp of Refuge,' professing to be a collection of fictions under the title of 'Old English Novelists,' will furnish interesting descriptions of the state of the country in the eleventh and twelfth centuries.

1070. Camp of Refuge.

'The townships were small, rustical, and wild; the fashion of their houses had little changed since the days of the ancient Britons. The houses, or huts, were of round shape, and not unlike the forms of bee-hives. They had a door in front, and an opening at the top to let out the smoke, but window to let in the light there was none. The walls were made of wattle and daub; the roofs of rushes or willow-branches cut in the Fens; but the better sort of house had stone foundations, rough stone pillars, and traves for the doorway.

'But these poor houses were not so comfortless within as might have been prejudged by those who only saw the outside. The hides of cattle, the fleeces of sheep, the skins of deer, and the abounding feathers of the fen-fowl, were good materials for good covering and warm clothing. Neither turf nor wood for firing were ever lacking in these parts; and the brawny churls, who came forth from the townships blowing their blast-horns, and brandishing their fen-poles over their heads, did not look as if they were scant of music.

'There seems also to have been some taste and civilisation about the inhabitants, for gleemen and minstrels were ever going from township to township, with their voices, and harps, and Saxon lyres.'

It may be interesting to us, who still make use of the pole, to know that 800 years ago our ancestors did the same; and we have an account of a young novice, going on his way from Crowland to Spalding, in the midst of the Fens. 'He carried a pole in his hand to leap the ditches and try the boggy ground; the upper part of his staff was fashioned like the staff of a pilgrim; the lower part was armed with a heavy iron ferrule, from which projected long steel nails and spikes. It was a fir-pole such as our fenners use in Holland, Lindsay, and Kesteven. When the autumn sun shone out brightly there was a pleasant and varied prospect in an occasional opening between the monotonous forest of willows and alders.

'The kingfisher flitted across his path, the wild-duck rose from the fen and flew heavenward; the heron raised itself on its long legs to look at him from the sludge; the timid cygnet went sailing away in quest of the parent swan.

'The novice had quitted the causeway, which for the most part was merry in summer, but a complete morass in the winter.

'The Isle of Ely was, to all intents, an inland island, being surrounded on all sides by lakes and meres, and broad rivers, which became still broader in the season of rain; there being few artificial embankments to confine them, and few or no drains or cuts to carry off the increase of water to the sea or Wash. The isle had its name from *Helig* or *Ely*— a British name for a willow, which grew in great abundance in every part of it, and which formed in many parts low, but almost impenetrable, forests, with marshes and quagmires under them and within them.

marginal note: 1150. Camp of Refuge.

'The whole isle was almost a dead flat, with here and there an inconsiderable eminence standing up from it. These heights were often surrounded by water, and when the autumnal and spring rains swelled the meres and streams and covered the flats, they formed so many detached islets. When were there in the world such eels and eel-pouts as were taken in the Ouse and Cam, close under the walls of the abbey at Ely? (3,000 eels, by ancient compact, do the monks of Ramsey pay every Lent to the monks of Peterborough, for leave to quarry stone in a quarry appertaining to Peterborough Abbey; but the house of Ely might have paid 10 times 3,000 eels, and not have missed them, so plenty were they, and eke so good.

'The streams, too, abounded with pike, and the meres and stagnant waters swarmed with tench and carp.

'Nor is there less plenty of water-fowl, and for a single halfpenny men can have enough for a full meal.

'Nor was there a lack of fish that came up the river to spawn.

'Of wild boars of the forest in the Fen the head only was served up.

'The wild buck was less abundant in the fenny country.

'It was also facile to snare the crane, the heron, the wild-duck, teal, and the eccentric and most savoury snipe; the swallow-kite, the swarth raven,

PETERBOROUGH CATHEDRAL.

the hoary vulture, the swift eagle, the greedy goshawk, and that grey beast, the wolf of the weald.'

The state of the country may be further illustrated by the following series of quotations from various sources. Dr. Adam Mercer, in 1505, does not take a more favourable view of our Fen country. He styles it, 'one of the most brute and beastly of the whole realm, a land of marshy ague and unwholesome swamps.'

'In 1620,' says Dugdale, 'certain undertakers drew up proposals, which were submitted to the Commissioners of Sewers, stating that they intended, without any tax to be levied on the country, effectually to drain the whole level and latitude of the Fens, as the same lie subject to their natural outfalls to the sea.' The undertakers were not able to fulfil their contract, because His Majesty (as Sir Cornelius Vermuyden says), for the honour of his kingdom, would not any longer suffer these countries to be abandoned to the will of the waters, nor let them lie waste and unprofitable. He did himself undertake, by a law of sewers, a great work of drainage. In this place I will insert a popular ballad, quoted by Dugdale from Armstrong's 'History of Lynn,' which possibly indicates the ordinary feeling of opposition to an extensive reform, and represents that which Tacitus calls the 'vitium parvis magnisque civita- 'Agricola.'

tibus commune, ignorantiam recti et invidiam,' *i.e.*, a feeling common to corporations small and great, viz., an ignorance and an envy of what is right; or, according to another old chronicle of the Fen, 'He who will do any good in sewaging must do it against the will of such as shall have profit in it.'

BALLAD.

<small>1620. Dugdale, History of the Fen, p. 391.</small>

Come, brethren of the water, and let us all assemble
To treat upon this matter, which makes us quake and tremble;
For we shall rue it, if it be true the fens be undertaken;
And where we feed on fen and reed, they'll feed both beef and bacon.

They'll sow both beans and oats, where never man yet thought it,
Where men did row in boats, ere undertakers bought it;
But, Ceres, thou, behold us now; let wild oats be their venture;
And let the frogs and miry bogs destroy where they do enter.

Behold, the great design, which they do now determine,
Will make our bodies pine, a prey to crows and vermin;
For they do mean all fens to drain, and waters overmaster;
All will be dry, and we must die, 'cause Essex calves want pasture.

Away with boats and rudders, farewell with boots and skatches,
No need of one or t'other—men now make better matches.
Stilt makers all and tanners shall complain of this disaster,
For they will make each muddy lake for Essex calves a pasture.

The feather'd fowl have wings, to fly to other nations,
But we have no such things to help our transportations;

We must give place—oh, a grievous case—to hornèd beast and cattle,
Except that we can all agree to drive them out by battle.

Wherefore let us all entreat our ancient water nurses,
To show their power so great as t'help to drain our purses;
And send us good old Captain Flood to lead us out to battle—
The twopenny Jack with scales on 's back will drive out all the cattle.

The noble Captain yet was never known to fail us,
But did the conquest get of all that did assail us.
His furious rage none could assuage; but, to the world's great wonder,
He bears down banks, and breaks their cranks and whirligigs asunder.

God Œolus! we do thee pray that thou wilt not be wanting.
Thou never saidst us nay; now listen to our canting.
Do thou deride their hope and pride that purpose our confusion;
And send a blast, that they in haste may work no good conclusion.

Great Neptune, God of Seas, the work must needs provoke ye;
They mean ye to disease, and with fen-water choke thee;
But with thy mace do thou deface and quite confound this matter;
And send thy sands to make thy lands, when they shall want fresh water.

And eke we pray thee, Moon, that thou wilt be propitious,
To see that nought be done to prosper the malicious;
Tho' summer's heat has wrought a feat, whereby themselves they flatter,
Yet be so good to send a flood, lest Essex calves want water.

1689.

Macaulay, in his 'History of England,' has given a graphic account of the inhabitants of the Fen at the close of the seventeenth century, from which we cannot infer that they were very much advanced in civilisation, or that the country was more habitable than at an earlier period.

'The mutineers were hastening across the country, which lies between Cambridge and the Wash. The road lay through a vast and desolate fen, saturated with all the moisture of thirteen centuries, and overhung during the greater part of the year by a low grey mist, above which rose, visible many miles, the magnificent tower of Ely.

'In that dreary region, covered by vast flights of wild-fowl, a half-savage population, known by the name of breedlings, there led an amphibious life, sometimes wading, sometimes rowing, from one islet of firm ground to the other. The roads were among the worst in the island.'

1754.

The following extract was copied from the Bible of John Brown of Chatteris, being one of many marginal notes: 'I, Carter Potto, after the distemper had raged in this kingdom for seven years and upwards, sold hay at $\frac{1}{2}d.$ per pound, which is 4s. 8d. per cwt., and could have sold it for 5s., but that I had promised I would not raize it no higher price, but would not sell it to nobody for no horses,

ELY CATHEDRAL.

but for cows. This was in the winter of the year of our Lord God 1754. At that time a great many parishes lost 1,000 milch and other cattel—Chatteris, March, Cottenham, Willingham.'

'In the winter time, when the ice is strong enough to hinder the passage of boats and yet not able to bear a man, the inhabitants upon the lands and banks within the Fens can have no help of food nor comfort for body or soul, no woman an aid in her travail, or partake of the Communion, or supply of any necessity, saving what those poor desolate places do afford, where there is no element of good—the air being for the most part cloudy and full of rotten harrs; the water putrid and muddy, yea, full of loathsome vermin; the earth spongy and boggy; and the fire noisome by the stink of smoky hassocks.' 1772. Dugdale, History of the Fen, p. ix.

The country became more dissatisfied with the state of the drainage; and in 1775 a meeting was held at the George Inn, Ramsey, by the proprietors of lands in the Middle Level to consider of a plan proposed for a general outfall to the sea and the better drainage of said lands—W. Fellowes, chairman. It was the opinion of the meeting that the only method for that purpose must be by running the water through the Tongs sluice, and that such run should be had at all times (provided there is a fall in the Ouse) until the water shall be one foot below 1775.

soil in the lowest lands of the said level. That the 16 foot, the 40 foot, the River Nene, and Bevill's Seam, be scoured out.

1793. In 1793, Arthur Young reports 'that numbers of sheep die of the rot when depasturing in the drier parts of the Fen during the summer months. The number also stolen is incredible; they are taken off by whole flocks; whole acres of ground are covered with thistles or nettles four or five feet high, nursing up a race of people as wild as the Fen.

'The few wretched inhabitants who live in the neighbourhood for the most part sheltered themselves in huts of rushes and lived in boats. They were constantly liable to be driven out of their cabins by the waters in winter, if they contrived to survive the attacks of ague, to which they were perennially subject. The East Fen was the worst of all; 2,000 acres were constantly under water in summer. One part of it was called Mossberry and Cranberry, from the immense quantity of cranberries thereon.'

1795. A thousand acres in Blankeny Fen, constituting the dales of Lincolnshire, was one of the most fertile parts between Lincoln and Tattersall.[1] They were let by public auction at Harecastle, and the reserved bid was 10*l.* for the whole area. About the middle of last century there were but two houses in the

[1] Journal of Agricultural Society, vol., 1847.

CROWLAND ABBEY.

whole parish of Dog Dyke, and these could not communicate with each other for whole winters round, except by boat, the only means by which the Fen sledgers could get to church. The entire breadth of Lincolnshire north of Boston often lay under water for months together.

CHAPTER IV.

CROWLAND ABBEY.—CAMDEN'S ACCOUNT.

CAMDEN's description of Crowland, in his 'Britannia,' may still further show the low estimation in which the Fens were held in former times. 'Crowland,' he says, 'lies among the deepest fennes and waters stagnating off muddy lands, so shut in and environn'd as to be inaccessible on all sides, except the north and east, and that by narrow causeys. In situation, if we may compare small things with great, it is not unlike that of Venice, consisting of three streets, divided by canals of water, planted with willows, and built on piles driven into the bottom of the fen, and joined by a triangular bridge of admirable workmanship, under which, the inhabitants report, is a pit of immense depth dug to receive the confluence of waters. Beyond this bridge, where the soil cements to solid ground, anciently stood the monastery—all round which, except where the town stands, it is so moory that you may run a pole into the ground to the depth of thirty feet; and nothing is to be seen on every side but beds of rushes, and, near the church, a grove of alders. It is, notwithstanding, full of inhabitants, who keep their cattle at a good distance from the town, and go to milk them in little boats (called skerries) which will hold but two persons. But their chief profit arises from the catching of fish and wild fowle, which they do in such quantities that in the month of August they drive 3,000 ducks into one net, and call their pools their fields—no corn grows within five miles of them. On account of this fishery and catching of fowls they paid formerly to the abbot and now to the King 300*l.* sterling a year.'

<small>Dugdale, History of the Fen, p. 210.</small>

Dugdale mentions the monastery of Crowland, and confirms the preceding account of its neighbourhood. 'By the inundation and overflowing of rivers the waters, standing upon the level ground, maketh a deep lake, and so rendereth it uninhabitable, excepting in high places, where the monks of Ramsey, Thorney, and Crowland reside; to which there is no access but by navigable vessels, except into Ramsey by a causey raised on the one side thereof.

CROWLAND BRIDGE.

Within the same precincts also Ely is placed, being an island seven miles in length and the same in breadth, containing twenty-two towns, encompassed on every side by fens and waters, and approachable only by three causeys.

CHAPTER V.

ST. GURLACH'S VISIT TO CROWLAND.

THE following is Dugdale's account of this visit: Dugdale, History of the Fen, c. 38, p. 179.

'The writer of this saint's life states:

'" In the middle part of Britain there is a hideous fen of huge bigness, which extends in a very long track even to the sea, ofttimes clouded with moist and dark vapours, having within it divers islands and woods, as also crooked and winding rivers. When, therefore, that man of blessed memory, Gurlach, had found out the desert places of this vast wilderness, he inquired of the borderers what they knew thereof. One amongst them, called Tatwaine, stood up amongst them, who affirmed that he knew a certain island in the more remote and secret parts thereof, which many had attempted to inhabit, but could not, for the strange and uncouth monsters and several terrors wherewith they were affrighted, wherewith Gurlach earnestly entreated that he would show him that place. Tatwaine, therefore, yielding to the request of that holy man, taking a fishing-boat, led thereunto; it being called Crowland, and in respect to its desertness known to very few, by reason that apparitions of devils were so frequently seen there. Not long after, St. Gurlach being awake in the night time, betwixt his hours of prayer, of a sudden he discerned all his cell to be full of black troops of unclean spirits, which crept in under the door, as also at chinks and holes, and coming in both out of the sky and from the earth, filling the air, as it were, with dark clouds. In their looks they were cruel, and of form terrible—having great heads, ill-favoured beards, rough ears, wrinkled foreheads, fierce eyes, teeth like horses, swollen ankles, preposterous feet, and hoarse cries; who with such mighty shrieks were heard to roar, and by-and-by, rushing into the house, first bound the holy man, then drew him out of his cell, and cast him over head and ears into the dirty fen; and, having so done, carried him through the most rough and troublesome parts thereof, drawing him among brambles and briars for the tearing of his limbs."'

CHAPTER VI.

ANECDOTES CURRENT IN THE LAST CENTURY.
SONG OF THE THREE REVELLERS.

THE hospitality and habits of the occupants of the larger mansions of the Fen country may be illustrated by two or three anecdotes current in the last century. Mr. Smiles, in his 'Lives of the Engineers,' relates that Mr. Rennie, in 1799, 'went to dine and stay all night with Sir Joseph Banks (then President of the Royal Society) at Revesby, near Tattershall, in Lincolnshire.' On this occasion he took an opportunity of saying to the principal butler that he hoped he would see to his postboy being kept sober, as he wished to leave before breakfast on the following morning. The butler replied, with great gravity, that he was sorry he could not oblige Mr. Rennie, as the same man had left Revesby sober the last time he was there, but only on condition that he might be allowed to get drunk the next time he came. 'Therefore,' said the butler, 'for the honour of the house I must keep my word; but I will take care you are not delayed for the want of horses and a postboy.' The butler was as good as his word. The man got drunk, the honour of

Smiles, Lives of Engineers, vol. ii., p. 155.

Smiles, Lives of Engineers, vol. ii., p. 156.

Revesby was saved, and Mr. Rennie was enabled to set off in due time next morning.

The following short story will illustrate the mode in which Fen justice was administered and awarded. A boy was brought before a baronet, a justice of the peace, and was convicted of poaching. A letter was given to him with instructions to take it to the governor of a neighbouring gaol. Within was the order written: 'Give the boy a dozen, and let him go.' It occurred to the culprit that he should like to see the contents of the letter, and on his way he opened it. When he arrived near the gaol he met another boy, and said to him: 'I have a note for the governor, and my time is precious; will you deliver it?' The substitute went, and was surprised at receiving a dozen lashes, which were duly administered.

A story of four noted whist-players, which obtained circulation, and was recorded in a provincial newspaper, may, perhaps, deserve notice, though we may hope it was not true. The tradition, which was currently believed to be founded on fact, was to the effect that after one of the four had died and been buried his companions disinterred the corpse and made it play dummy. This grotesque tale was embodied in the following verses, as a parody on 'Alonzo the Brave,' by Mr. Rawnsley, in the days when the writings of Monk Lewis were popular:—

The Three Revellers; or Impiety Punished.

In the bleak, noxious fens which to Lincoln pertain,
    Where agues exert their fell sway,
Where the bittern hoarse moans, and the sea-mew complains
    As she flits o'er the watery way;

While in strains thus discordant the natives of air
    With shrieks and with screams the ear strike,
The toad and the frog, croaking notes of despair,
    Join the din from the bog and the dyke.

Midst scenes which the senses annoy and appal,
    Sad and sullen old Holbeach appears,
As if doom'd to lament her hard fate from the Fall,
    Like a Niobe wash'd with her tears.

From fogs pestilential that hover around,
    Fraught with gloom and with pain and disease,
The juice of the grape best repellant was found,
    Source of comfort, of joy, and of ease.

At the Checquers, far fam'd, to quaff their delight,
    The burghers, both ancient and young,
With smoking and cards pass'd the long winter's night,
    They laugh'd, and they joked, and they sung.

Three revellers left when the midnight was come,
    Unable their game to pursue,
Repair'd, most unhallow'd, to visit the tomb
    Where enshrinèd lay one of their crew.

For, he, late departed, renown'd was at whist—
　　The marshmen still tell of his fame—
Till death struck the spade and the cards from his fist,
　　And spoil'd both his hand and his game.

Dark and damp was the night; through the churchyard they prowled
　　Like wolves by fierce hunger subdued.
'Gainst the doors they huge gravestones impetuous hurl'd,
　　Which recoil'd at such violence rude.

From the sepulchre's jaws their old comrade uncas'd—
　　How dreadful the tale to relate!—
Uprear'd 'gainst the wall, on a table was placed
　　The corpse, in funereal state.

By a taper's faint blaze and Luna's pale light,
　　That would sometimes emit them a ray,
The cards were produced, and they cut with delight
　　To know who with Dummy should play.

Exalted on basses, the bravoes kneel'd round,
　　Exulting and proud of the deed.
To Dummy they bent with respect most profound,
　　And said: ''Tis your turn, sir, to lead.'

The game was commenc'd, when one offer'd his aid,
　　And affected to guide his cold hand;
Another cried out: 'Brave Dummy, well play'd!
　　I see you've your cards at command.'

Thus, thoughtless, they jeer'd, devoid of all grace;
　　Loud sounds shook the walls of the church;
When Dummy sank down, and a Fiend in his place
　　Shriek'd dismal: 'Haste, haste, save your lurch!'

Astounded they star'd; the Fiend disappear'd,
  And Dummy again took his seat.
They deem'd 'twas but fancy, nor longer they fear'd,
  But swore that old Dum should be beat.

'Eight to nine was the game,' Dummy's partner call'd loud,
  'Speak once, my old friend, or we're done.
Remember our stake—'tis my coat and your shroud.
  Now answer and win—Can you one.'

'What, silent, my Dummy, when most I you need!
  Dame Fortune our wishes has cross'd—'
When a voice from beneath howl'd: 'Your fate is decreed!
  The game and the gamesters are lost—'

When, strange, most terrific, and horrid to view,
  Three spectres through earth burst their way.
Each one seized his partner, his arms round him threw,
  And vanish'd in smoke with his prey.

No wretch sacrilegious, since that fatal hour,
  The chancel has dar'd to draw near,
Lest the spectres again should exert their fell power,
  And drag him to punishment drear.

Ofttimes, it is said, at the dead of the night,
  When gamesters and drunkards reel home,
The Revellers three with old Dummy unite
  To beckon the sots to the tomb.

Then busy they seem as, intent on their game,
  While the gazers affrighted stand by,
On a sudden the spectres appear clad in flame,
  And, shrieking, away they all fly.

1800.

We have now arrived at the conclusion of the first division of our subject—the general condition of the Fens. The desultory quotations which have been made disclose a dark and dreary prospect. At the same time many efforts had been made in the way of improvement, which gave ground to hope that better things were in store for the inhabitants. The attention of Royalty had been turned to the consideration of the country. The great proprietors and others had shown an interest in the subject of drainage. Some valuable cuts and rivers had been made; and

1799.

we find one at Ramsey, bearing the respected name of Fellowes, M.P., who advocated the true principle of getting a lower outfall to the sea. The beginning of a new century seems a convenient point at which to make a break in my narration. I shall be able in the next portion of the work to state facts which I have received by tradition from an older generation, or which have fallen under my own observation. The change which took place in the country from and after this period will be more apparent. The results of the engineering talent employed, and of the vast sums of money spent on various schemes of reclamation, are evident in the enormous increase of the produce of the soil, as well as in the improvement of health, and in the comfort and happiness of the population at the present time. These are acknowledged facts; and we may confidently assert that the material results are among the great marvels which have marked the progress and advancement of this prosperous century.

PART II.

CHAPTER I.

NOTICES OF WHITTLESEA MERE.

The great level of the Fens comprehends in round numbers, as already stated, 750,000 acres. In the time of Charles II. it was placed in the hands of a Corporation for purposes of reclamation and drainage. It was subdivided into the Middle, North, and South; and one of the important objects of the exertions of the present century has been to obtain a separation of these levels. Another great object was the drainage of Whittlesea Mere and the lands adjoining. It is to this district more particularly that I wish for the present to draw the attention of the reader. The earliest notice respecting it that I have been able to find occurs in Domesday Book, where it is stated that in 864 it was granted by Walphere, king of Mercia, to his newly-founded monastery of Medesham Stede, now Peterborough. In 1507 Henry VII. granted the office of Keeper of the Swannery on the Mere to

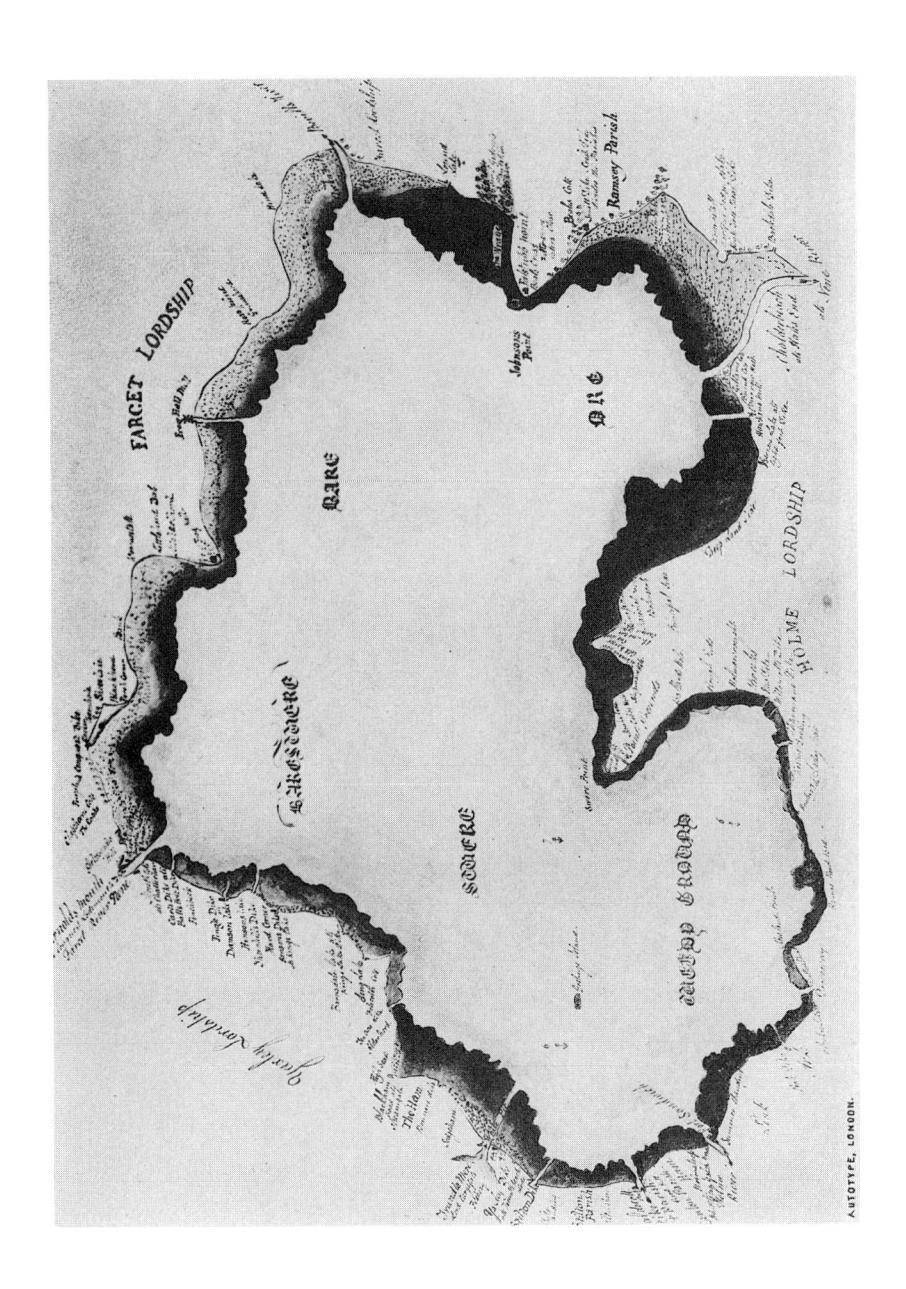

MAP OF WHITTLESEA MERE.

CONNINGTON CASTLE, 1800.

David Cecil for a term of seven years. In 1662 Charles II. granted the same office, with that of Bailiff and Keeper of the Mere to Edward Earl of Sandwich. According to the survey of Bodger, made in 1786, its waters covered 1,870 acres. In its ordinary state it was $3\frac{1}{2}$ miles long from east to west and $2\frac{1}{2}$ broad from north to south. Its depth was from 2 to 7 feet. Sir John Rennie, in his survey of 1835, found a diminution in the depth of the Mere, and also in its area. The change he attributed to the improved drainage and outfall. Mr. Walker found by his soundings in 1844 that Whittlesea Mere was still further diminished in extent and depth.

1786.

CHAPTER II.

CONNINGTON AND RAMSEY.

As Connington and Ramsey border so nearly on the Fens, and as they both possess some antiquarian interest, it may be worth while to make a short digression on their local history. Connington was anciently held of the Honour of Huntingdon. Within a square inclosed by a fosse or ditch there are traces of an ancient castle. This was the seat of

Turkill the Dane, from whom it descended to Waltheof (son of the Earl of Northumberland), who married Judith, the daughter of a sister of William the Conqueror, through whose eldest daughter it came ultimately to the Royal family of Scotland; for she married for a second husband David Earl of Huntingdon, who afterwards ascended the throne of Scotland. Through a female line Connington descended to Robert Brus, and passed from his younger son to Sir Robert Cotton, the antiquary, who was an intimate friend of Camden. A mansion was built by Sir Robert Cotton, which stood at the west end of the church, facing the north. Sir Robert removed from Fotheringay Castle to this mansion the room in which Mary Queen of Scots was beheaded.[1] The colonnade was likewise removed, and was placed in a situation similar to that in which it stood at Fotheringay. Dr. Stukeley describes a visit which he made to Connington in the course of one of his journeys in 1724. 'I was concerned to see a stately old house, of hewn stone, large and handsome, in dismal ruins. The deserted *lares* and the genius of the place had fled. A poor cottage or two seem to be the whole town, once in the possession of the kings of Scotland.'

[1] Mrs. Markham's 'History of England.' Dr. Stukeley's 'Itinerary' Notice of Fotheringay.

CONNINGTON CASTLE, 1875.

Sir John Cotton, great-grandson of Sir Robert Cotton, Camden's friend, finding the family seat in a ruinous state, and having a predilection for the seat at Stratton in Bedfordshire, took down the Connington mansion, leaving only a stone colonnade in the front. Its place is now occupied by a modern farmhouse. Sir John Heathcote, son of Gilbert Heathcote, one of the founders of the Bank of England, and Lord Mayor of London, purchased the Manor of Connington of the heirs of Sir R. Cotton in 1753 for the sum of 2,500*l.* This Gilbert Heathcote was knighted by Queen Anne, and afterwards (1733) created a baronet. He was the original Sir Andrew Freeport of the 'Spectator.' *[margin: Camden's Britannia.]*

In 1800 J. Heathcote, Esq., commenced draining and improving the estate of Connington, under the superintendence of J. Burcham, of Connisby in Lincolnshire. Some idea may be formed of the state of the district from a fact frequently stated to me by George Thornhill, late M.P. for the county. He once got into a gunning-boat from the windows of the dining-room on the ground-floor at Connington Castle, and paddled off afloat to shoot coots in the lower part of Connington Fen. This boat of the district was about 10 feet long, drew 3 inches of water, and was propelled by one person with a sprit or pole. The flood-water of the neighbouring brook was unusually high. The farm horses on the soft lands used to plough with wide boards attached to their shoes by straps.

CHAPTER III.

RAMSEY ABBEY.

<small>Camden's Britannia.</small>
RAMSEY—that is, Ram's island—is separated from the firm ground on the west by clayey quagmires, about two stones'-throw in breadth. The fens render it inaccessible on any other side. The place, which was formerly reached by ships, conveyed by gentle gales, between the pleasant banks of a sluggish stream, is now—thanks to the expenditure of great pains and much money in the filling up of swamps by wood, sand, and stone—approached by persons on foot by a solid causeway, nearly two miles long, and of considerable breadth. The island was covered with alders, beds of green sedges and bulrushes, and long before it was inhabited various trees grew there, and especially large quantities of elm. Now it appears a fine arable soil, smiling with corn—the woods being destroyed—planted with gardens, enriched with fruits, abounding in pastures and beautiful meads, exhibiting in spring a charming prospect. The whole

island presents a picture of lovely flowers in great variety. It is besides enriched with fens abounding in eels, and with marshes breeding various kinds of fish and water-fowl.

Dr. Stukeley mentions 'Ramsey Abbey, famous for its wealth, where every monk lived like a gentleman.' There is little left now but part of the old gatehouse. When I visited it I saw in the yard the neglected statue of the famous Alwyn, who was the founder, and was called Alderman of all England. I take this to be one of the most ancient English pieces of sculpture now extant. The keys and ragged staff which he holds in his hand are the insignia of his office. The inscription on the founder's statue is: '*Hic requiescit Alwinus incliti regis Edgari cognatus, totius Angliæ Aldermanus et hujus cœnobies miraculosus.*' At the dissolution of the monasteries the revenues of Ramsey Abbey amounted to 1,987*l.* per annum. In 1540 the demesnes and lands of the Abbey, with meres and lakes belonging to it in the parish, were granted to Sir Richard Cromwell for 4,963*l.* His son, Sir Henry, repaired and built the manor-house. Sir Oliver Cromwell, son to Sir Henry, lived here many years, after he had sold his estates at Hinchinbroke. Two coheiresses sold the estate to Colonel Titus, M.P. for the county, who left the estate to his wife and

1724. Dr. Stukeley's Itinerary.

daughter. The surviving daughter left it to two servants, who sold it to Coulson Fellowes, Esq., about the year 1730. It descended to his son, William Fellowes, and afterwards to his son, William Henry Fellowes, the father of the present owner, who came into possession in 1837. The present mansion was in great measure built by the present E. Fellowes, Esq., M.P., under the superintendence of Mr. Blore.

I may add that the old walls of the refectory, with their beautiful arches, still remain in a good state of preservation in the Abbey. There is also an old oak door, with the initials of Henry Cromwell upon it; and some of the old walls and buttresses still form part of the Abbey. The statue of Alwyn, the founder, was said to have been discovered in a pond in the time of Charles II., and at the beginning of the present century it was placed in the Abbey for safe-keeping. In the muniment-room is a very interesting and valuable collection of deeds relating to the Abbey.

BOAT-GATE OF WHITTLESEA MERE AND THE BURE.

CHAPTER IV.

THE BURE AND SETTING TRIMMERS.

IN 1805 a small cutter was first brought into Whittlesea Mere, and so many persons have at different times sailed in her and enjoyed very happy hours that I am induced to give a detailed account of her first appearance in this locality.

Mr. Preston came from the Broads or lakes in Norfolk in a cutter, which he called the *Bure*. She drew two feet of water, and had a large mainsail, foresail, and jib. There was a cabin, where eight persons could dine, an after-cabin, sleeping-berths, and a kitchen. The water in Whittlesea Mere gradually sinking, Mr. Preston could not get away. He therefore offered his vessel for sale, and it was bought by Lord Sandwich and J. Heathcote, Esq., for 120*l*. For many years parties from Connington were constantly made for sailing and fishing. The dead-lines were set with eel-hooks and trimmers, which were attached to a long line of stakes, stretching away usually in a curve toward Swords Point. The boatmen, early in the morning, baited the hook at the end of a long line, so fastened to the stake as to unwind at the slightest pull. The trimmers were examined in the course of the day by the visitors, who were punted along in a flat-bottomed boat. It was worth while to send to the Ouse for gudgeons as a bait when a good day's sport was required. Pike of 5 lb. to 12 lb. weight, eels 2 lb. to 3 lb., perch 3 lb. to 4 lb. were frequently caught.

In a letter written to me by Rev. Thomas Rooper, in November 1864, he says—

'I always, during my college life, spent a week with a friend during August near Whittlesea Mere. Old Berry received us, who at that time rented the Mere. We paid him 7s. each per day for board and lodging, and spent our time in shooting flappers, moor-hens, halfen, &c. One day we were astonished at the arrival of the "Bure." The owner, a Norwich clergyman, invited us on board, and stated that he lived all the summer in his ship, cruising round the coast and navigating the rivers, and in his course that he had stumbled on Whittlesea Mere, which he was about to leave the following day. I told him there was a great gathering to take place in the course of ten days, and if he could stay I would introduce him to half the county—who were about to assemble there. He replied that the ship was his house, and gladly accepted my offer. The meeting took place, and his vessel attracted great admiration. The following day he requested Berry to procure two strong cart-horses to draw his vessel through the dykes to the river. Berry replied they were too shallow to float his vessel till the rains fell in November. " Well," he said, " I am as well sailing here as anywhere else."

'About two months afterwards I went to see my friend. "Oh," he said, "this is perfect banishment. I have seen nothing but peat-barges since you left."

'Yours ever,

'THOMAS ROOPER.'

CHAPTER V.

FEN SCENERY AND ARTISTS—LETTER FROM PROFESSOR SEDGWICK—MIRAGE.

IT is gratifying to a fenman that he can recall to mind the great interest taken by visitors in our country. Many are now living who have made the commonest public-house their temporary residence for the purpose of shooting snipes. I can myself remember some circumstances under which persons of note have communicated their impressions when visiting our low country. In 1844, when I went as one of a deputation to ask Lord Monteagle to take charge of the Middle Level Bill in the House of Lords, he consented, but with the expression of great regret at the prospect of being instrumental in draining away the waters of a lake where he had spent so many happy days. Mr. P. Dewint and Mr. George Fripp stayed with me some days. Both made sketches in the neighbourhood, and were delighted with the scenery. I commissioned a friend to invite Mr. David Cox to pay me a visit, and make a few sketches in the Fens ; circumstances, however, did not permit him to come, but he stated in reply that he would rather sketch in the Fens than in the Highlands of Scotland. Mr. E. W. Cooke, R.A., came here on more than one occasion, and was an enthusiastic admirer of all that he saw. He collected the *drosseras*, various rushes, butterflies, and insects. He packed them in a large hamper and sent them to London. He subsequently exhibited in the Royal Academy a picture called the 'Deserted Mill in the Snow,' which was sketched in the neighbourhood, and is now in my possession.[1] The

[1] Mr. Cooke, after a visit made to me in 1875, kindly sent me a sketch of a Fen Mill made many years ago, which I had intended to introduce as a frontispiece. For reasons which it is unnecessary to give, I have thought it better, however, to substitute for it his sketch of a 'Deserted Mill in the Snow,' for the publication of which also I have his permission. The letter which accompanied it so well expresses his appreciation of Fen scenery that I have requested his permission to introduce it into my narrative :

Glen-Andred, Groombridge, Sussex: Sept. 27, 1875.
'My dear Mr. Heathcote,—
'I send you a sketch I made in the Fens, the best I have

admiration of the Fens expressed by these distinguished artists may to some be a matter of surprise, and its terms may seem to be merely agreeable hyperbole and compliment; but those who have studied the principles of Dutch art, and know the basis on which the fame of that school permanently rests, will acknowledge that the Fen country, when

with me, of those charming little draining-mills, which once abounded in that interesting country. I shall be glad to lend it to you for publication in your volume; perhaps it may do as a frontispiece, and then it will not seem out of place among your other subjects. It can be reduced in autotype to your own size, exactly, or perhaps it may be three-quarters of an inch larger than the rest. I send it direct to you, so that you will do what you deem best with it. Connington Church comes in, and the old sails take off somewhat of the formality of the woodwork of the vangs.

'I never was more surprised than when I saw the present state of the Fen-land, as compared with its former condition, when Whittlesea Mere was quite a scene of interest to the visitor; both to the painter, sportsman, and the naturalist. One now looks in vain for that broad expanse of water, reflecting the grey, passing clouds, and margined with vast masses of *Arundo phragmites*, sedges, and other marsh-loving plants; a dark vista tempting the sportsman to penetrate somewhat into the decoy and then preparing in his duck-boat for many a shot at the several wild-fowl which used to abound and enliven that Dutch-like scene. Then how fine were those bright, broad leaves and cup-like flowers of *Nymphea alba* and *Nuphai lutea* through which we poled our little punt! After the many sojourns I had made in Holland it was no wonder that I so thoroughly appreciated the characteristic features of the Fens. The towers of the Cathedral, the neighbouring spires, and the numerous and highly-picturesque water-mills and their clicking machinery—all these were charms for which we now seek in vain, but which we can never forget.

'Pray tell me if the sketch will do, and, with kind regards to your circle,

'Believe me,
'Yours very truly,
'E. W. COOKE.

in an undrained state, teemed with the beauty that was especially embodied in the works of Teniers, Cuyp, Hobbema, and Ruysdael. Here were found the same long, flat lines, the same richness of local colour arising from an exuberant flora, the forms of cattle reflected in the drains, the mills, the dwellings, dress, and habits of the inhabitants, the boats which navigated the rivers, and the same conspicuous atmospheric effects, contingent on the mists and exhalations, rising and falling above the swampy surface. All these objects are included in the term 'picturesque,' and from time immemorial have been a source of inspiration to those who desire to represent the real appearances of nature; thus rivalling other districts which are more generally admired and are often supposed to exhibit a greater beauty and variety of scenery.

An extract from a letter written to me by Professor Sedgwick gives an account of a happy day passed on Whittlesea Mere in 1809. 'I went to join a merry fishing-party. By way of bravado I started from a jolly supper at St. John's College, and walked all night through to Whittlesea Mere, arriving there about seven hours and three-quarters after I made my start from the college gates. When I arrived at my friend's house he was not up. Times are changed since. The load of eighty years

REGATTA ON WHITTLESEA MERE, 1842.

and the condition of the heart compel me to abstain from any but the most gentle exercise.

'Yours ever,
'A. Sedgwick.

'March, 1865.'

In 1826 Whittlesea Mere was quite dry, and every fish perished. They lay like heaps of snow on the north shore. The season was dry, and a large proportion of the bed of the Mere was without water. In the mud were large cracks and fissures; and when about a hundred acres of water remained a great hurricane of wind came and blew most of it into the cracks and fissures, and it disappeared. Many tons of eels, carp, pike, and perch were taken. The water returned in the winter, but there was no fishing for five or six years. The Mere, however, was stocked with fish from the rivers, especially from Bevill's Seam.

In June 1842 there was a regatta on Whittlesea Mere. Barwick made a sketch of it at the time, and several oil-paintings representing it are said to be extant. There was a terrific thunderstorm, with torrents of rain, while preparations were making for dinner. The provisions were soon afloat; a canoe was upset, and a man is shown in the sketch to be holding it over his head in place of an umbrella. My illustration of the scene was copied from the oil-picture and given to me by Mr. Dawson Rowley.

<small>'Land and Water'; also 'Norwich Argus,' July 13, 1872.</small>
He also showed me an old picture of a pike taken in Whittlesea Mere, weighing 52 lb., with an inscription on the panel: 'Such were the giants of Huntingdonshire in the olden times. The pike and the great copper butterfly (*Lycæna chrysophanus dispar*), now extinct, whose metallic wings glistened in the sun, are to be seen, alas! no more. The resting-place of the Harriers (circus) is gone, while over the habitat of many a fen-fowl Ceres pours her golden gifts.'

The old painting of this grand fish was exhibited at Kensington Museum in 1873, among Mr. Buckland's collection.

The following is an account of a mirage observed at Wisbeach by Mr. G. Millar:—

<small>From the 'Nation' newspaper.</small>
The phenomenon called 'mirage' is not very common. There was one seen May 29, 1873, in the form of a beautiful lake spread out a few miles distant. The illusory waters were of a bluish grey colour, and, being apparently raised above the level, presented the perspective of a Mere of considerable breadth; but this was not a dull expanse, there were variously-formed indentations, islands dotted here and there, pollard willows inverted, and reflections of tall poplars and elms on the glassy surface.

There was half-an-inch of rain on the previous Monday. The conditions generally were favourable to evaporation.

CHAPTER VI.

FACTS RELATING TO LANDS ADJOINING WHITTLESEA MERE.

I SHALL now string together a few facts relating to the lands adjoining Whittlesea Mere, with no observation except that they were communicated to me by inhabitants. Mr. Russell used frequently to take up his quarters at the sign of the Whittlesea Yacht, from whence he went in search of the birds found in that neighbourhood. On one occasion he had been shooting, and sat down to rest in Holme Fen. A bird settled near him with rather an unusual flight. He shot it, and it turned out to be 'the great grey shrike' or 'butcher-bird.' He has, in the same locality, found the eggs of the common snipe and starling. W. Coles shot seven or eight bittern or butter-bumps in a day. He once took two alive in a bow-net—while walking over it their feet had become entangled in the meshes. Setting out in company with my brother we shot in one morning seven bittern in a field of Holme Fen two or three hundred yards from New Dyke. I sank in the bog above my waist and remained there till ropes and assistance were procured from a distant cottage to extricate me. Shooters in gunning-boats used to make a circle and surround coots. They shot them as they flew up and passed the boats. W. Coles's father has killed sixteen to twenty at a shot, by stalking and firing a large gun. In a similar way he has shot seven, eight, or ten wild-ducks. The season for this sport was between November and March. Wild-ducks were only occasionally shot in Whittlesea Mere, and unless they were actually killed they would dive and were lost. Lord Erskine made use of this fact in a simile, which he applied to the minorities in which Ministers were frequently left in 1810. He said: 'They were like wild-ducks shot in a large lake—it was easy enough to knock them down, but very difficult to get them out.' Peter Phillips has seen in Walton Fen ten or twelve yards of dyke white with snakes, twenty deep, one over the other. They were attracted out of a plantation of dry sedge to look for frogs' spawn. He has also seen a dyke full of frogs. Their croak about sunset was very loud and heard all over the Fen. Adders and snakes were very numerous. A price was offered for every adder killed and produced, and in one year seventy were brought in to claim the reward. In the autumn, and during the winter, starlings used to assemble in large flocks. They frequently rested on the reeds, and did much damage. When on the wing their flight is graphically described by Dante:

> E come gli stornei ne portan l'ali,
> Nel freddo tempo, a schiera larga e piena;
> Così quel fiato, gli spiriti mali
> Di quà, di là, di giù, di sù gli mena.[1]

—' And like a numerous flock of starlings winging their flight in winter, so does the blast, now here, now there, now high, now low, whirl the bad spirits in many a varied form.' The crested grebe was seen, the didapper, the bearded titmouse, brown buzzards, ash-coloured falcons, ruffs, and rheas. The kite, with his yellow claws, the forked-tail kite, *Falcon milvus*, Le Milan Royal Buff, or in Scotland called gleads, the red feather of whose tail was famous for wings of salmon-flies. These birds were commonly seen soaring over Monks Wood, and twenty-seven have been counted at one time.[2] They have now become quite extinct in these parts, and I have been informed that they got their food from the marshy ground, and when the swamps were drained the birds disappeared.

[1] 'Inferno,' canto v., lines 40-44.
[2] 'Down the Road,' by C. Reynardson.

CHAPTER VII.

THE OLD FEN MILL.

The Fen mill has become a relic of the past, and is almost entirely superseded by modern machinery. It is gradually falling to decay, and the time is approaching when an explanation will be required to illustrate its use and operation. The fields of a district were divided by ditches, all communicating with a large drain, which ran up to a mill turned by four sails. A wheel of large circumference (round which horizontal boards were placed at right angles), revolving in a narrow space of wood-work communicating with the drain, scooped up the water from the lower level, and delivered it into the main river. The higher level of water was here protected by banks, between which a stream, flowing with a fall of three inches per mile, found its way to the sea. When the land was very wet and the winds ceased to blow, the mills could not work, and the drainage was at a stand. Such would sometimes be the case for weeks together. Mrs. Moysey, widow of one of the oldest inhabitants of the parish of Connington, stated to me that she lived close by the four-score mill, and that the whole country used to be drowned for weeks. She remembered the water coming into her

MILL USED FOR DRAINING THE FENS.

MILL USED FOR DRAINING THE FENS.

cottage and floating the ground-floor. Her husband carried the children to the bank and walked them to the mill. Sisman, afterwards bailiff to J. Heathcote, Esq., used to draw on his fen-boots when he left his bed in the morning, the floor of his cottage as well as the legs of his bedstead being covered with water for weeks together. Bricks were piled on the hearth on which to light a fire. Whether we look at the old Fen mill within or without, it is equally interesting, equally suggestive of past habits of Fen life, and of pictures of the Dutch school. I will describe two which now occur to my recollection. On entering one there is a dusky gloom reminding us of Rembrandt's colouring. A massive wooden spindle stands in the centre of the mill, and terminates in a large set of cogs at the top, which communicate with the arms of the sails. A tarpaulin is drawn from side to side. In one dark corner is a bed and a wooden chest. There is a fireplace, but no egress for the smoke. Such was the dwelling in which a family permanently lived. Another mill forms a subject of one of my illustrations. Its body is dilapidated and the planks are falling to decay. Two of its arms have disappeared, and the remaining two are in a shattered condition. There are several openings, which disclose large massive beams and daylight between them. The old brick-work which was the channel for the water is tumbling to pieces. The wheel in many places is broken, and the nave with the radiating spokes still remains. The three long poles by which the mill was formerly turned to the wind complete the picture.

CHAPTER VIII.

SNIPE-SHOOTING—THE PLOVER—THE DECOY.

SHOOTING snipes was one of the great events of the season. They came in November, usually in flocks, but ever afterwards when disturbed rose singly. At that time they were always in the best condition. We frequently started at seven o'clock to shoot, and in the sloppy places had to break through a thin skimming of ice. The ground on which it was most likely to find them was in the short-cut sedge and boggy pools, where the cattle had fed during the summer. We considered a good day's sport to vary from six to fifteen couple. My keeper, J. Goodlad, who was a very good shot, and often went in pursuit of them, never exceeded twenty-five couple, which he recorded as his best day. The ditches were jumped with a pole. A cess or lump of turf was placed in the middle of the ditch, the pole was placed upon it, and ten to fourteen feet was traversed easily.

The plover is a beautiful bird, which used to make its appearance at appointed seasons. They flew about in great numbers, especially in the skirt lands. They laid their eggs on the ground, and in consequence of the speckled colour they were not very easy to find. Old Crane, a labourer, used to go over all the fields, and was singularly expert in finding them. They were taken in great numbers, and their price varied from twopence to fourpence or sixpence each. In the 'Gentleman's Recreation' (Part IV. c. 27) I find the following account of these birds:—'Plovers used to fly in exceeding great flocks together; they generally come to us about September, and leave us in or about March. In frost or cold weather they seek their food on such lands as lie near or adjoining the sea. In thaws and open seasons they go higher into the country. They delight much to find ploughed lands, especially if sowed; and, having fed, they presently seek out for water to wash their beaks and feet. When they sleep they do not perch on anything, but crouch and sit on the ground, as ducks or geese. They only sleep in calm weather; otherwise they pass most of the night or morning in running up and down to seek for worms, as they come out of the ground, and then they always make a little cry, and keep close together, for at daybreak they always unite in a body, and so depart. If in their flight they chance to espy any others on the ground they usually call to them, and if they refuse to go they make a stay, expecting some booty. They are most easily taken in October.'

A visit to the Decoy was a favourite pastime for our friends. We made our way to Mr. Skelton who lived in a lonely farm-house, at a short distance from the Decoy. We were often told 'The wind is not right. You cannot see the covey to-day.' But in the event of our having permission he gave us a piece of lighted turf, with instructions to breathe upon it; otherwise the ducks would be aware of our approach. We were then conducted in a mysterious way so that we should enter the enclosure upwind. Strict silence was enjoined. The Decoy itself included a space of several acres, dedicated to the purpose, and left to run into a wilderness of alders, sedge, and reed. In the centre was a pond, in which swam tame ducks, trained from their egg-shell to deceive their species. Several ditches or pipes were cut with a slight curve issuing from a large pond, about three or four yards wide at the entrance, and thirty to fifty yards long. This terminated in a hoop-net, like the purse of a drag-net, and at its termination was about two feet wide. Across the pipe, poles, being driven into the ground, were bent towards each other and netted over, decreasing in height from the entrance to the end of the pipe. A series of reed-screens on one side of the pipe were placed at such an angle that the ducks could not see the walkers. In each of the screens a little dog-hole

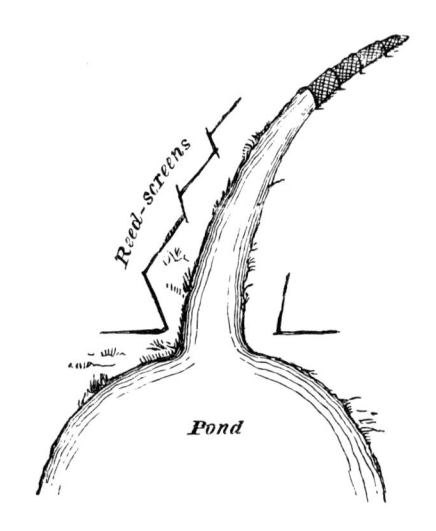

Reed-screens

Pond

was left, about a foot from the ground, through which a dog was trained to jump, show himself, and return to his master, who gave him a piece of cheese. The wild duck is an inquisitive bird, and his instinct directs him to swim towards the spot where the dog shows himself. The dog repeats the exhibition of himself at each remaining screen, and the ducks in like manner follow him. The dog was then ordered to lie still, while Skelton showed himself at the end of the pipe next the pond. The birds flew forward into the purse-net, which was removed with such birds as were caught. The time of catching was by law from June 1 to Oct. 1. Teal and widgeon were taken between October and March.

Frank Coles, now occupying a farm in Holme Fen, has told me that Skelton, who established his decoy about the year 1815, stated to him that for the first three or four years the decoy was drowned, and he caught no ducks. In the following year he took two hundred dozen in seven days. The price of ducks in Leadenhall Market was usually eight shillings a couple.

CHAPTER IX.

FEN IN TIME OF FROST.

ONE of the most interesting varieties of Fen pleasure was an excursion along the rivers when frozen. I started from Connington one morning at seven, with the Rev. Mr. Eastwick, putting on our skates a quarter of a mile from the house. The morning was cold, and the east wind pretty strong against us.

MILL WITH SKATERS DRAWING A SLEDGE.

The ice was good. The scenery of the Fen rivers, at all times beautiful, in the eyes of those who appreciate Dutch art, is peculiarly so in the winter. The mills, of varied form and colour, are conspicuously placed on the banks; cottages also, such as modern thought has learned to despise and calumniate, with willows and trees denuded of leaves, make most picturesque groups; and then there are cattle standing by old hovels built by the owners. Boats, eel-trunks, frozen up in the ice, slackers all closed up and useless, little gunning-boats with their sprits lying on the bank, stacks of reed by the side of the river, groups of figures skating, some drawing sledges loaded with sedge—all these are objects of beauty and interest.

We passed Chatteris along the 40-foot, and reached a small public-house at Welches Dam. The wind was high, and the river then became wider. Before making a fresh start we asked at the inn for a small glass of brandy, which was refused by the publican, who said: 'No, no,—you be the exciseman!' We prevailed at last, and continued our journey till opposite Ely Cathedral. We then turned back and reached our starting-place about seven in the evening.

In the year 1799 Francis Drake, an officer of the Bedford Level Corporation, is said to have put on his skates at Whittlesea and crossed both the Middle and South Levels to Mildenhall without taking them off—a distance of nearly fifty miles. Mr. Waddelow has heard this fact spoken of from his childhood, and he has seen the grandson of William Drake, who stated that it was frequently mentioned as a feat in his family. While on the subject of skating, let us suppose that we have put on our pattens prepared to enjoy the fresh, breezy air and the genial sun of a fine winter's morning on Whittlesea Mere. We pass up one of the lodes and find a wide expanse of frozen water. The ice upon the Mere varied much from year to year, and often took a different phase during the same frost. There was the hard, black, smooth ice, which, by a little skimming of snow with slight thaw and subsequent frost, would be made white. A gentle breeze during the time of freezing made knotted ice. There was also the anchor ice, so called when it froze under the surface and on it at the same cold temperature. Sometimes a high wind would roll up water and mud, and the surface became very rough. There was the bright ice, which when hard and slippery was called 'glib.' The cracking of the ice was a curious incident, making a loud noise which was heard a long distance at night. We will now imagine the ice to be perfect, and that there is a great gathering for a race. About the

SKATERS ON FEN DRAIN.

SKATING ON WHITTLESEA MERE, 1835-6.

SKATERS AND SLEDGES

OLD WOMAN SELLING CHESTNUTS

intended place of starting a great crowd is collected. There is an old woman sitting 'with chestnuts in her lap' and roasting others in an old grate. A Dutch oven is by her side, and a crowd of buyers round her close by. On one side a rude, oblong box on bones, and drawn by two dogs, imported a little gin for those who were thirsty. Many thousands are collected together, and groups are skating in various directions. But the larger number are occupied in superintending that portion of the ice which was marked out for the course. During a frost the occupation which excited the greatest interest in the country was these skating races. A good surface of ice gave as good a prospect of competition and as happy a holiday as the day of the Derby. The candidates for the prize came from the surrounding towns and villages of the Fens, and much rivalry was excited between them. The reputation of former winners still lives in our recollection, and I may say that the names of Needham, Tomline, Green, Dyer, Turkey Smart, Sharman, Skelton, and Smith are still 'familiar in our mouths as household words.' The prizes offered were a cocked hat, a pig, or a purse containing from 1*l.* to 20*l.* The pairs who competed were matched by ballot, and all the races were run off by pairs, till the two last contended for the prize. I have endeavoured to ascertain the opinion of the neighbourhood as to the greatest pace at which ice has been traversed, and the result of my enquiry is that one of the fastest miles on record was performed by John Gittan of Nordelf, at Padnal near Ely. The ice was good, and the wind in his favour; he got into full speed before reaching the starting-post, and performed the distance of a mile in two minutes and twenty-nine seconds. I have also been informed, on credible authority, that Turkey Smart was backed for money to skate a mile in two minutes. He frequently tried, but never actually succeeded. But he only exceeded the two minutes by two seconds. The ordinary pace of a fast skater is one mile in three-and-a-half to four minutes. The success of the best skaters is found to culminate at the age of twenty-two, and they are soon afterwards obliged to give way to the efforts of younger men. During the very long frost of the winter of 1835–36 I fitted up a green-baize dress lined with flannel. I carried it while skating till I had selected some spot for sketching. I then put on my Esquimaux dress, and sat under the shelter of reeds. Some of my sketches bear marks of the severity of the cold by showing the crystals into which the water froze when floated on the paper. The scenery was in many respects peculiar to the country, and well

GROUPS ON THE ICE.

RACE ON WHITTLESEA MERE

REED HARVEST.

CUTTING REED.

CUTTING SEDGE.

STACKING REED

worthy of description. During frost, when the rivers and drains were frozen, and when highland work was slack, a winter harvest commenced in the fens. The cutting of reed and sedge was a busy and interesting scene. A gang of ten or twelve labourers, in rich, warm, stuff jackets and high fen-boots, were employed in cutting white reeds fourteen feet high, with brown feathery flowers in filaments at the top. The reeds were laid in bundles, piled in sledges, which ran on marrow-bones, and were removed along the ice to the entrance of the lodes or rivers, where they were stacked and left for further removal when the river navigation was open. The sedge was mown, and the scenes presented during the harvest days were exceedingly picturesque.

CHAPTER X.

A STALKING-SLEDGE.

THE mode of stalking after wild birds was curious. It may be worth while to compare the practice of the Fen man with an account given in the 'Gentleman's Recreation,' chap. 4, part 5, describing a similar process. My illustration represents a man kneeling on a long raft or sledge about sixteen feet long by three or four feet broad. Four marrow-bones are fixed at the bottom of the sledge. In front is a fence of upright reeds, kept together by two or three cross-sticks. The barrel of a long duck-gun projects through the reed fence about three or four feet. The stock of the gun, at the extremity of which is a boss of soft leather, rests on dry sedge. A coarse piece of brown leather covers the lock. A man dressed in a leather coat, a fur cap, and a pair of large fen-boots, kneels at the hinder part of the sledge and punts himself along by two short sticks terminating in iron prongs. Long, narrow lines of islands of sedge stretched for many yards across the Mere, and on these ducks and wild-fowl frequently rested. By means of the sledge the birds could be approached without alarming them. The gun discharged a pound of shot, and a great number of birds were frequently killed. The following is the passage in the 'Gentleman's Recreation,' chap. 5, page 127 :—' Forasmuch as fowl do frequently lie remote from shelter, so that the fowler is deprived of a shot; therefore by the assistance of a stalking-sledge he may command a shot at pleasure.' I need not enter into minute details which are given relating to the stalking-horse, the artificial wheel-barrow, and the stalking-tree. The stalking-hedge

STALKING SLEDGE.

approaches nearest to the stalking-sledge on the Mere. The stalking-hedge should be two or three yards long, a yard and a half high, and made in small wands and bushed out in the manner of a true hedge, and certain supports or stakes to bear it up from falling, when you take your aim to shoot, and this is to be carried before you, for your shelter from the fowl. To conclude the chapter, observe the caution that 'these several sorts of engines are to be used early in the morning and late in the evening, and they are more proper for water than for land fowl, for when the sun is up its reflections soon discover the imperfections in your engines which the water better hideth.'

Before I finally quit the account of this frozen period, I will mention one circumstance related to me by Mr. Richardson of Peterborough. When the ice was very clean and transparent he remembers to have watched a large pike swimming beneath it. The fish seemed frightened and moved onwards. He followed and after a long skating chase the pike was tired. The ice was broken, and he was taken out of the water. He was found to weigh twelve pounds.

CHAPTER XI.

BIRDS, FLOWERS, INSECTS.

MR. WELLS's gardener, Whybury, made a valuable collection of insects, some of which he sent to the British Museum. He was the only person who could find the copper-butterfly. It was very rare, and he knew where to look for it. On one unfortunate occasion he accompanied some strangers who came from London. They made their excursion, and went afterwards to the public-house for refreshment. There they took advantage of the feelings of an open heart, and prevailed upon Whybury to tell his secret. From that time he ceased to have the monopoly, losing thereby a source of great emolument. In the village of Holme there are still persons who were instructed by Whybury, and who possess boxes and trays full of these curious insects. I have seen there the swallow-tail butterfly, which has now disappeared. It was seen seven or eight years ago. The peacock-butterfly is marked with an eye such as we see on a peacock's tail feather. Some of the moths measured five or six inches when stretched out. The death's-head moth has a head like a monkey and wings of considerable length. An extract from a letter written to me by Rev. Thomas Rooper, who was an experienced observer of the Fens, gives an interesting account of his research:—' Most of the rare butterflies were found on the banks of Whittlesea; amongst them, the swallow-tail and the copper butterfly, so scarce that not above three or four were to be met with in the course of a year. Naturalists made journeys from London on purpose to find them. Their habitat was between Holme Lode and Swords Point. I never saw but one. In the middle of the lake there was a small island on which people were in the habit of landing to take tea. Berry gave me this account, but not a vestige of it remained in my time. I will now make a short notice in respect of botany. I once and only once found the English cranberry; the *locale* was on the right side of Holme Lode. In the same neighbourhood grew the *Ophrys Lœsilii*. In the same part of the marsh grew the *Typha minor*. I have added the names of a few more common: *Parnassia palustris, Marsus Ranæ (hydrocharis), Solidago, Lythrum Salicaria, Pilularia globutifera, Senecio sylvaticus, Calamintha acinius, Stellaria (cerastoides* and *glauca), Salix (herbacea* and *aquatica), Myrica gale, Equisetum palustre*, and three species of *Drosera*. All these I met with when I was last on a visit to you.

'Yours ever,

'THOMAS ROOPER.'

Dr. Paley, in his 'Flora of Peterborough,' says: 'The immediate neighbourhood of Peterborough is very rich in wild flowers on the Fenside, and particularly those of the *Endogen* class. Of this great family are the *Hydrocharis* (or frog-bit), *Sagittaria aliena*, *Butomus* (the flowering rush), *Sparganum* (burweed), *Typha* (reedmace or bullrush).'

Among the more conspicuous of the *Exogen* plants are the *Bottomia palustris* (water-violet), *Nymphæa lutea* and *alba* (yellow and white water-lily), *Lythrum Salicaria* ('long purples' of Shakspeare[1]). *Scutelaria* (or skull-cap), *Myosotis palustris* (the water forget-me-not), *Achilles Pharmici* (the sneeze-wort), *Lysimachia* (*nummularia* and *vulgaris*), money-worts, and *Spiræa ulmaria* (the meadow-sweet).

The dykes and railway-cuttings in the direction of Ely and Holme, Holme flats, and the site of the now historic Whittlesea Mere, are sure to reward careful research. Most of these teem with bog plants. The *Carnatia palustris*, with many others, have wholly disappeared. The *Umbellifera juncacene* (*cyperacene* and *promnens*) are common; the great *sinum* and *Cicuta virosa* (the water-hemlock), *Stirpus palustris* (or true bullrush), *Arundo phragmites* (or common reed). There is a *fen*

[1] Hamlet, act iv. scene 7.

weed (*Anacharis alsinastrum*) which grows in the drains and rivers of the Fen and very much impedes drainage and navigation, as it checks the natural flow of the water to the sea. Its origin and the way in which it was introduced into this country is not generally known. The notice on the subject which I have inserted was given to me by the Rev. Thomas Rooper, who lately died at a very advanced age. He had always paid much attention to botanical subjects. Mr. Rooper had a slip of the Anacharis, which he presented as a curiosity to the Botanical Professor at Cambridge. It was planted in a pond, and was for a time forgotten. It found its way, however, into the Cam river, and in some strange way was propagated all over the Fens. The story was told, but it is more satisfactory to have the following account sent to me by Mr. Rooper:

In his letter dated November 23, 1864, he says, 'This weed found its way into England some twenty-five years ago, and was reported to have been found in a small pond in Sir George Staunton's park. I made an excursion to see it. Sir George gave me some specimens. I sent half my treasures to the Curator of the Botanic Gardens, Cambridge. He planted it in a pond, from which it escaped, and in due time got into the river, stopped the current, and flooded the neighbourhood. But it may be doubted, after all, whether that was its origin, for the next year it appeared in the river Nene, and five years afterwards I found it in a large pond in Mr. Chetwode's park. This pond had been cleaned out before, and no account could be given of its being there. I sent a specimen to Sir William Hooker. It is now common over England. This *hotomogeton* differs from all others in two respects—unlike its congeners it sinks when cut and takes root at every joint. Swans are very fond of it.

The *Vallisneria spiralis* is not a native, it abounds in the Rhine, and is remarkable for the flux and reflux of the sap like the blood in the human frame.

'Yours ever,

'T. R.'

CHAPTER XII.

CUTTING TURF.

THERE was one source of profit to the owners of Fen soil which is worthy of notice. This was turf-cutting. About three, four, or five feet below the surface a hard, fibrous substance rests on the clay, and it was the custom to cut it into bricklike shapes and sell it for fuel. The price was about ten

LOADING TURF AT STORY'S BRIDGE.

shillings per thousand pieces, and they were generally used in the cottages of the country. They were dug out of holes, which were left at intervals as pits to hold water in the rainy season, and to afford a resting-place for snipes. In the neighbourhood of Chatteris and other places a space was often set apart and allotted for the use of the poor. We have all frequently met, in parts remote from the Fens, a cart filled with 'Warboise turf,' and we have all wondered what could be the profit of such a cargo. Connected with the history of the turf-field, there is a curious episode of the dry year of 1871, an occurrence which might have led to most disastrous effects. In the parish of Connington some weeds were burned by the side of a fen-ditch, and the fire was permitted to smoulder till the turf below the surface became ignited, and the fire was communicated to the adjoining fields. The travellers along the Great Northern Railway in the night-time during that year will remember the little hillocks of flame that burst from the surface of the soil, and over a considerable acreage made a brilliant display. No efforts on the part of the occupier availed to extinguish the burning over the farm, and for some time the buildings and stacks were threatened by its gradual approach. After a conflagration which continued for several weeks, the rain at last fortunately extinguished it.

CHAPTER XIII.

VALUE AND PRODUCE OF LAND.

UNDER this head some facts may be mentioned which will, in a striking manner, illustrate the immense rise in the value of land in the Fen country, consequent on the great drainage operations. Inundations have at all times been common, but the damage done by them in earlier periods was far less than at present, as farming is now carried on in a more expensive manner. While the drainage was so bad little wheat was sown in the outlots. An old farmer, Mr. Joseph Little, used to say he never fallowed his land but when Providence did so, by a flood or breach of bank. The next year's produce, after a summer's fallow of that sort, was always a good crop of first-rate quality. It made no difference how the land had been farmed before the flood, the white water from the hundred-foot river was so renovating.[1] In South Lincolnshire, in 1817, 75,000 acres lay under water for the greater part of the year. The wretched state of the lands may be inferred from the fact that, seventy years since, 1,000 acres in Blankeney Fen were let annually at Harecastle, and the reserved bid was 10*l.*

[1] Smiles's 'Lives of Engineers,' vol. ii. chap. v.

for the whole area. During the last century 400 acres of land, together with buildings which cost 300*l.*, were sold for 150*l.* Again, 600 acres were sold for 10*l.* In fact, all the corporation land on Burnt Fen sold for the amount of the taxes. Under the old mill-drainage the taxes were 4*s.* 6*d.* per acre, in addition to the Eau Brink taxes—with a most uncertain drainage. Sisman offered one hundred acres of fenland to J. Heathcote for 100*l.*, but the latter did not think it worth while to accept the offer. Sisman lived to be his bailiff, and enjoyed his greatest confidence; he transacted much of the business of the estate, and had the management of the farm, though he could neither read nor write. Mr. Jones, agent for Mr. Fellowes, stated to me that 80 acres of land near Ramsey were sold before the drainage for 904*l.* They are now worth 40*l.* an acre. He also told me that another estate near Marshland, which sold for 7,000*l.*, has lately been purchased for 57,000*l.* It will be interesting to know a few facts bearing on the value of lands adjoining Whittlesea Mere, as well as of the Mere itself, previous to 1844; and carefully to refer to statements which will be made hereafter (Chap. VI.), with a view to showing the great improvement which resulted from the drainage. Whittlesea Mere was hired by

Coles and his father up to the time of reclamation.[1] The old fishery was rented at 30*l.* per annum. 200 acres of reed border, called shoals, round the Mere, which produced 1,000 bundles of reed, was worth 5*l.* an acre. The sedge which grew outside the reed was cut once in three years and the crop formed about 1,000 bundles. This land was worth 1*l.* per acre; 1,300 acres of Fen held with the Mere had an average value of 2*s.* an acre, for joint purposes of sedge-cutting and rough pasturage—total value 1,350*l.* Reed was cut from the beginning of December till March.

The Second Part of our proposed account is now concluded, and we have arrived at the important period of 1844. The value of the land is a fair test of public opinion as to the efficiency of existing drainage systems; and in many cases we have seen how utterly valueless it was considered. Much discussion had taken place in respect to improvements, and the mind of the country was ripe for a more extensive change. The period we have now reached was on the eve of the employment of great engineering skill, and of the adoption of measures which ensured a real and efficient drainage, and contained the germs of complete and ultimate success.

'Journal of Agricultural Society,' vol. 21, p. 134.

PART III.

CHAPTER I.

VARIOUS SCHEMES RELATING TO THE DRAINAGE OF THE FENS.

A RAPID glance at the various Acts of Parliament which have been passed at different periods will afford us indications of a continued endeavour to improve the locality and expressions of a desire, on the part of all classes of society, to combine and co-operate for the benefit of the Fen country.

1292. The ancient outfall of Ouse was by Wisbeach to the sea. Its name was Ousbeach. The commission of 21 Edward I. ordained the waters of Well to be sent by Wisbeach to their former outfall. At that time the Haven of Linne was but six perches wide.

1342. Waters passed uninterrupted by Salter's Lode to Linne.

1422. New Powdike cut from Salter's Lode.

1490. In the reign of Henry VII. John Morton, Bishop of Ely, Lord Chancellor of England, for more speedy conveyance of waters out of the Isle of Ely, cut a river 40 feet wide 14 miles long to Guytterin.

1605 Was the date of Lord Popham's undertaking.

1618. A session of Court of Sewers held at Huntingdon, which reported that undertakers project to drain.

1634. Francis Duke of Bedford made the old Bedford river 70 feet wide, 21 miles long, and a sluice at each end. Bevils Leam 40 feet wide, 10 miles long.

1638. King Charles I. made an undertaking to construct a bank on the south side of Moreton's Leam to Wisbeach, and a cut below to the sea.

1641. William Earl of Bedford made an undertaking to lower the sea outfall. Sir Cornelius Vermuyden reported: 'By guidance of nature, and art as an assistant to it, we shall prevent mischief for the future.'

1650. Undertakers propose to make a sluice at Hermitage and Denver.

1652. Denver sluice erected by Sir Cornelius Vermuyden.

1653. Tongs Drain Cut.

1795. Eau Brink Act passed.

1821. Eau Brink Cut opened.
Original Estimate 38,098*l*.
Accounts certified by Sir John Rennie 149,115*l*.

1799. Sir John Rennie's plan for Catchwater Drain.

1844. Middle Level Act—Walker, engineer.

1857. Estuary—Victoria county projected.

1860. Ouse Outfall Act, 2 mile cut.

1861. Act passed for the separation of Middle and South Levels.

1863. Inundation of Marshland. Siphons erected. Removal of shoals above Lynn.

1874. Act passed to restore the sluice.

CHAPTER II.

DRAINAGE OF WHITTLESEA MERE.

THE year 1844 was a most important epoch in Fen affairs. A general agreement had been come to by the residents of the district that something should be done, and that Whittlesea Mere should no longer exist as 'The Great Southern Lake.' But much difference of opinion existed as to the mode of carrying the drainage of the Mere into effect. Various schemes had been suggested.

Mr. Charles Margatts, a resident at Huntingdon and an owner of Fen property, called a meeting in 1838, which assembled at the Woolpack Inn, Connington Lane, to consider the subject. A large and influential party wished to employ the engineers of the country. But before giving an account of the measures then adopted, I will notice a meeting of the proprietors of Welmore Fen, which was held at Horncastle in 1799. Resolutions were there passed to authorise Mr. Rennie to investigate the subject and report. It was stated on this occasion that much good land was lost for purposes of agrculture; that in the neighbourhood of Downham Fen the harvest-men in certain seasons were obliged to stand on a platform when reaping, and carry the corn in boats to drier parts; that some farmers rowed through their orchards to gather the fruit from the trees; that a large portion of Littleport Fen was let for 1s. an acre; that stock in summer were turned out among the reed and sedge and were not seen for weeks together; and that in Marshland Fen the soil was so soft that wooden shoes or flat boards were nailed to the horses' feet to prevent their sinking in the ground. Mr. Rennie at that time proposed a scheme of drainage; but the only part of it that was executed was the Eau Brink Cut, by which $5\frac{1}{2}$ feet additional fall was gained at St. Germain's bridge.

Sir John Rennie had in 1799, and again previous to 1838, proposed to make a catch-water drain below the range of hills to the west, running along the border of the lowlands to Peterborough. His great principle was that no flood highland water should pass into the Fens, and that the outfall should be at Wisbeach. Vessels of large burthen would then be enabled to float up the river Nene to Peterborough. Lord Fitzwilliam was very anxious that Sir John Rennie's scheme should be adopted. Sir John Rennie came to Connington in 1838, and walked with me some time on the terrace, explaining his views at great length.

Mr. Tycho Wing also desired that the drainage should be by the river Nene. I had a most interesting ride with him in the same year, by the Dog and Doublet, to Wisbeach, and to the extremity of the guide banks. It was curious to observe the effect of the tidal deposit of soil and the first growth of vegetation. The warping process was then going on: rows of low thorns or small faggots were fastened across the level area of sand. At every reflux of the tide a small deposit was made and a surface of soil created. The sea-thistle seemed to be the first plant that could establish its existence there. As the soil became deeper other plants made their appearance, and a prospect was held out that in the course of time there would be a surface of great fertility. In connection with Mr. Tycho Wing's views on the drainage of the Middle Level, he explained to me many circumstances which attended the first opening of the Cut below Wisbeach. One I remember, of great importance, because it was the decisive test of success. Sir John Rennie and Mr. Tycho Wing had pledged their money and their reputation that the scheme should not fail. The population of the country was angry, irritated, and incredulous. It was the great day of opening. There was an unusually high tide, and it seemed doubtful whether the banks would stand the pressure. At one critical moment the sea water was all but over the bank; a little more and there would have been a general inundation. In the furious temper of the people Mr. Rennie and Mr. T. Wing considered that their lives would be in jeopardy, and of this they were so fully persuaded that a small boat was kept in readiness, by which, in case of necessity, they intended to make their escape to America. Both Mr. Rennie and Mr. T. Wing had much to say in favour of their scheme, and I had to make my election between the rival engineers. The abstraction of fresh water, and the intense opposition which was certain to arise in the Middle Level, induced me to co-operate with Mr. Walker and the Commissioners. A general measure was agreed upon, which resulted in the Middle Level Act of 1844. The Lands of the Middle Level were taxed for the purpose of drainage to the amount of 200,000*l.* Under a subsequent Act, a further tax was imposed of 230,000*l.* The outfall was carried six miles further down the Ouse, and an additional fall of six feet was gained. The Marshland Cut was eleven miles long and forty feet broad, having an average breadth of seventy feet at the top. The cill of the sluice was laid six feet below datum (or the ordinary low-water mark at Lynn) in order to take advantage of any future contingent fall. I do not intend to enter into the details of the contest which beset the preliminary stages of the Middle Level Bill in the several rural districts. The want of funds, the slow apprehension of engineering truths, the conflict of opinion, the unfortunate misunderstanding with the Sutton and Manea district, are still remembered. It is sufficient to say, that much time and labour were required to overcome these difficulties, and to obtain the necessary agreement between the contending parties to send up a Bill for the consideration of Parliament. I will instance one day's work which I did myself. In the month of November 1842 I sent a hunter forward to the forty-foot bridge and galloped across Holme Fen, where I mounted another and proceeded to March. There was a long debate, and I could not leave till the important decision was arrived at. I left the Griffin Inn as the clock struck five. At Story's Bridge it became dark; the black, soft places in the Drove could not be discerned. I was therefore obliged to dismount and lead my horse, till I reached Holme Road between ten and eleven o'clock. At last a Bill was drawn and sent to London. The discussion was transferred then from the orators of the country to the forensic talent and ability of the Bar, and to the decision of an intelligent Committee, of which Mr. Philip Pusey was Chairman. When Mr Walker's scheme was contested in the committee-room of the House of Commons I remember that Mr. Austin, in his opening speech, took exception to it as being limited and partial. Mr. Walker had proposed a large and comprehensive scheme, which embraced the separation of navigation and drainage. The Commissioners adopted only one portion of it, which was the Sixteen-mile Cut, the Commissioners undertaking to clean out and deepen the rivers of the upper country. Mr. Austin denounced the scheme as a 'mongrel.' The term was generally accepted by the opposition, and formed the staple of many a subsequent effective attack. In a very warm corner of a committee-room in the House of Commons overlooking the Thames I sat for twenty-two days next Mr. Fryer, of Chatteris, who was at that time Chairman of the Commissioners. Mr. Talbot, our counsel, once came to us, and spoke of his notion, when about to receive evidence from the Fens, that they were the seat of ague and fever, and that the inhabitants would bear marks of general bad health. He expressed his surprise to find such robust and healthy-looking men as our Chairman, and regretted to admit that he and his colleagues of the long robe were the cadaverous parties.

The Act at last passed both Houses of Parliament, with some mutilation, and became law. One of the first operations under its authority was the cutting of the Engine Drain, with a view of carrying away the waters of the Mere. The cutting was fifty yards wide, and eight or ten feet deep, near the termination of the Holme Lode, which meets one of the main rivers at the engine-house. A clear way for the water was first made on each side of a plot of ground, which was ultimately the central and deepest part of the channel. This was at last cleared away, and a wooden stage was erected, from which the black soil and mud was wheeled to the bank. Solid clay is found here at a depth of from six to twenty-five feet. A hard gravel road has since been made for a distance of two or three miles by the side of the drain. A further excavation was made for the space of some hundred yards; the clay taken out was removed in trucks along a temporary tramway, and the adjoining fields were covered with clay to the depth of four to six inches.

CHAPTER III.

APPOLD'S PUMP.

1850.

I PASS on now to the immediate results of the Middle Level Act, and I will try to recall some of the circumstances of this important year. The Rev. E. Bradley was an attentive observer of all that took place about that time, and he recorded his impressions in the 'Illustrated London News.' His papers I have occasionally consulted. One of the first important measures was the erection of Appold's Pump, at the head of the Engine Drain, where the waters of Whittlesea Mere were to be discharged into the river, to be conveyed from thence to the sea. Those who visited the machinery department of the Crystal Palace will remember that one of the chief objects of attraction was Appold's centrifugal pump. In the illustrated catalogue it was stated that the pump contained one gallon, and discharged its contents 1,400 times in a minute; that it could do 73 per cent. duty, and was adapted for the discharge of a large quantity of water at a low lift. It had no valves in action, and was fitted for a tide pump. Though the performance of the pump afforded amusement, a strong opinion was expressed by some of our eminent engineers that for practical purposes it was useless, and would prove to be nothing more than an ingenious toy. W. Wells, Esq., of Holme Wood, determined to try it on a large scale, to drain upwards of 3,000 acres of land. Messrs. Easton and Amos were employed to erect it. The wheel, from which the pump derives its name, is 4 feet 6 inches in diameter. When set in motion the troubled water rises to the top of the sluice, and is forced over the gauge-boards in a roaring torrent, falling with a discharge of 1,652 gallons of water in a minute. When the machine works under a 5-foot lift the quantity discharged is $74\tfrac{1}{2}$ tons per minute. By removing two or three of the gauge-boards and diminishing the lift to two or three feet the volume of water discharged per minute is 101 tons—a quantity that would cover an acre of land to the depth of an inch. The pump is connected by a simple wheel-gear to a steam-engine of 25-horse power, working on the high-pressure expansive and condensing principle with 2 cylinders. The boiler is of simple construction, affording a large amount of heating surface. Its pressure is 3,500 tons, being 35lb. to the square inch. After an interval of 25 years, it may be an interesting subject of enquiry whether the Fen proprietors have consulted their own interest in adopting the principle of the centrifugal pump, for the drainage of their respective districts, in preference to the scoop-wheel. The latter is supposed by many engineers to be the most economical with a given steam-power, and to be capable of discharging the largest quantity of water in a given time, especially when there is a high lift. It is said that there is less friction, that no water escapes backwards, and that all power is exerted in the direction of the discharge. I have been credibly informed that in Majorca, Scotland, and other places the centrifugal wheel has been taken down to make way for the scoop-wheel. It was a great day of triumph when we were satisfied that the Engine Drain was completed and the pump was in working order. A luncheon was given by Mr. Wells in honour of the opening, and the repast was laid out in the engine-room.

Mr. John Fryer (chairman), Mr. Wells, Mr. Appold, and several other Commissioners were present. The room was decorated with flowers, evergreens, and reeds (the produce of the shoals); banners were hung round, and conspicuous among their mottoes was the following happy quotation from Byron, in allusion to the different aspect now presented by the country from that of the time when it was covered with water:

> ' We see, we recognise, we almost deem
> The present fiction and the past a dream.'

In 1850 the water finally left the bed of Whittlesea Mere dry. It flowed out by a small cut of the New Middle Level Drainage at Foleaster Point on the north-west side. As the water sank nets were dragged for weeks, and tons of fish were taken out; among them were pike from 5lb. to 20lb. and perch from 3lb. to 4lb. At last there was left an acre covered with fish 1½ feet deep. The bream, roach, and chub were not considered worth the trouble of removing. A few were buried, and thousands rotted on the surface. There was a second catch of eels in the mud. Great numbers of people came from a distance, and walked about with flat boards attached to their shoes, and they made a great spoil. In 1852 there was a flood; the banks gave way, and Whittlesea Mere was again covered with water. The engineer came down and calculated the time which would be required to lay the Mere dry again. The engine discharged the water, and the prediction in point of time was exactly verified.

CHAPTER IV.

THE STRATA BELOW THE MERE. THE NUT DEPOSIT.

Mr. J. Lawrance was present when Whittlesea Mere became dry; and he carefully superintended the boring and examination of the different strata. On the surface were a great many perfect fresh-water shells; in fact, the alluvial soil at the top was much composed of broken fragments of shells. This rested on peat, in which were found the skulls of a wolf and a wild-boar. Twelve feet below there was a marine deposit, and sea shells were found in great abundance. It was here that the skeleton of the grampus was discovered. About 4 feet below this surface there was a deposit of black leaves, closely compressed among which were a great number of nuts. This deposit extends all over the Fen country— even as far as the estuary.

It is generally asserted by naturalists that the antiseptic property possessed by peat soil is necessarily destructive of vitality in any seed that has lain in the subsoil during the formation and accretion of the peat. A case, however, occurred while the construction of the Great Northern Railway was in progress through the Fen district which may at least raise a doubt. An account of it, with the correspondence that ensued, is worthy of a place in a work purporting to record the general phenomena which were observed during the drainage of the Fens. The line passed for a considerable distance through the stems and trunks of a submerged forest, over which the peat had accumulated in the course of the thousand or more years since the sea broke over the flat, to the depth of three or four feet. The forest was composed chiefly of oak, ash, and willow, with an undergrowth of hazel. Under the stool nuts and acorns were found in large quantities, perfect in form and maturity, thus furnishing evidence of the time of year at which the inundation had occurred. Inside and out, however, the nuts were almost uniformly of a deep bronze colour. One day the Rev. J. Nowers—now Rector of Yelling, Hunts, but then employed as chaplain to the labourers on the line—observed among a handful of nuts some which appeared to have enough substance in them to admit of the possibility of germination. Mr. Nowers' letter will speak for itself. A correspondence took place at the time between the Rev. W. Rooper, to whom the nut that is said to have sprung from one of those kernels was consigned, and the late Sir William Hooker on the subject. Sir William, while consenting to give the little plant a place in the Royal Gardens at Kew, where it shortly perished, expressed a very decided opinion that, strong as the testimony was, it must yield to an established physical law, and he placed the nut in the same category with the 'mummy wheat.' The correspondence has not been preserved; but on Mr. Rooper's application, Mr. Nowers has kindly re-written the account, which, with the opinion of the present Curator of the

Royal Gardens (to a great extent in accordance with that of his late father), I am permitted to publish :—

'Yelling Rectory, St. Neot's : June 21, 1875.

'Dear Mr. Rooper,—In reply to your enquiries respecting 'the nut,' I have pleasure in giving the following particulars. The original from which I believe it to have sprung was found among many more in Connington Fen at about 3 feet six inches below the surface. I had picked up several, which, though in appearance perfectly sound, contained nothing in the shell. Some, however, were heavier. These I replaced in the cutting in the peaty soil, threw some surface earth over them, marked the spot, and awaited the result. I am sure that no human being knew that I had deposited the nuts in the cutting; and I may observe that all the shells were perfectly black or of the deepest possible bronze. It was in the spring and warm. I found a few weeks afterwards that a nut had germinated and put forth four tiny leaves. I mentioned the circumstance to you, and we decided to remove it. I took it carefully up, with the broken or open shell, out of which it had vegetated and placed it in your greenhouse, where it put forth two more leaves ; presently you had it removed to a place prepared and enclosed with wire in your orchard, where it remained for a

year or two and made some little but sickly growth.
It continued, in fact, to be a singular stunted little
plant while in your care. On leaving Ripton you
determined to ask Sir William Hooker, with whom
you had been in correspondence on the matter, to
allow it a place at Kew, where it was transferred. I
at the same time wrote a full account of the transaction for Sir William Hooker's inspection. I am
now writing entirely from memory after the lapse of
25 years, but the main facts are indelibly impressed
upon my mind, and I have no more doubt of the
reality of them than I have of my own existence.'

'Believe me, dear Sir,

'Yours very sincerely,

'JAMES H. NOWERS.'

Dr. Hooker, in reply to an enquiry from Mr.
Rooper whether he concurred in his father's, the
late Sir William Hooker's, opinion, that it was impossible that germination could have taken place under
the conditions, writes as follows:—

'Royal Gardens, Kew: June 1875.

'My dear Sir,—While unhesitatingly discrediting
the story of the "mummy wheat," I cannot go so far
as to regard it as impossible that nuts should retain
their vitality for many years in bog earth. There is,
however, no positive evidence of anything of the

kind, nor even approximate evidence worthy of the name. It would require the testimony of a careful observer, trained to scrutinise such phenomena, and acquainted with every step in the progress to substantiate such a fact. Like the sea-serpent, the more ships that are put to sea the more seldom is it observed, and as miracles disappear under education and strengthened reasoning powers so do a long class of once-credited phenomena. You, perhaps, know the history of the best-authenticated case of preserved vitality—that of the raspberry-seeds taken out of a Roman tomb and said to have germinated, and produced a crop of raspberry-canes, as vouched for by Lindley and a host of credible men. There was no doubt as to the seeds taken from the tomb being raspberry-seeds, nor was it doubtful that they were sown, and that raspberries grew up where the sowing had taken place. The seeds were seen and examined by hundreds of people at a meeting of the Horticultural Society. One acute man took some of the seeds home, and discovered that every one had the germ destroyed and could not have grown. He further showed at the time, what no one else seems to have noticed, that the seeds from the tomb were exhibited in an open flat paper tray, and that along with them was handed round a similar open flat paper tray of fresh raspberry-seeds for comparison. These were both handled, probably, by hundreds of people, and in all human probability some few fresh seeds got out of one tray into the other. Of all the people present Professor Henslow alone had the sagacity to appreciate this source of error on the spot, and was able to vouch for it, as also that the tomb seeds were destroyed and could not have grown.

'Yours very faithfully,
'J. D. HOOKER.'

'The Rev. W. Rooper.'

CHAPTER V.

RELICS FOUND BELOW THE BED OF THE MERE.

AMONG the relics were large circular water-vessels in common pottery-ware, and one of finer material, rather grotesque, of mediæval date. There was also a rude axe and another better formed. Near the clay were stags' horns and bones, and in the gravel a brow antler. Also a long iron sword of rude workmanship, and one of finer make with an inscription in gold letters. It may now be seen at Peterborough. There were also bones of the Arctic bear, and others of an Arctic type, of the primæval ox (*Bos longifrons*), and the teeth of the mastodon. One of the greatest curiosities discovered when Whittlesea Mere was laid dry was the fossil skeleton of the grampus, which is now in the possession of Mr. John Lawrance of Elton. The head is in length about 2 feet 6 inches. The forehead is flat. The length of the creature, including the vertebræ and tail, is about 40 feet. Large bones terminating in a fan-shaped bone on each side indicate the fins, one on each side of the face. The jaw-bones show great strength. Above and below in each are 11 holes in which are arranged 11 strong teeth. One of the teeth was shown to Professor Owen, who pointed out its similarity to the tooth of the bear, but affirmed it to belong to the grampus. On each side of the vertebræ 11 bones slightly curved show the ribs. Between the bones of the vertebræ are circular plates, the purpose of which was to make the whole length flexible. This voracious creature is mentioned in the 'Encyclopædia Britannica' under the head of 'Mammalia,' and there is also a full account of it in Owen's 'British Fossil Animals and Birds.' It is described as the *Phocæna crassidens*, or thick-toothed grampus—one of the *Cetaceæ delphinidæ;* and as the most complete skeleton of a cetaceous animal among the British fossil mammalia. A second specimen was discovered in the year 1843 in the great Fen of Lincolnshire beneath the turf, in the neighbourhood of Stamford, and it is now to be seen in the Stamford Institution. It belongs to the dolphin tribe, and is of the short-jaw or porpoise genus. The surface of the bed of the Mere was indented with wide cracks and fissures. In these were seen large roots of the *Nymphæa alba* and *N. lutea*, the flowers of which used to look so beautiful floating on the water. Mr. Walker, the engineer, told me that in taking the soundings across the Mere, in the centre from east to west, he found that the level of the bottom varied only as the curvature of the earth's surface, i.e. one inch per mile. About the middle of the lake was found, in 1851, a boat, in one piece, cut out of the trunk of an oak, embedded in silt. The boat was of rude construction, the thwarts being fastened by wooden pegs. The oak had become black, but the wood was hard and sound. The boat was 27 feet long, $3\frac{1}{2}$ broad. Some nuts were found lying inside it. An interesting silver relic was also disinterred, of a boat-like shape, resting on an elegant hexagonal base. All the ornaments were of silver-gilt, and most elaborately and delicately made out. The whole is in beautiful preservation. It is furnished with one lid. The vessel has been conjectured to be a salt-cellar, but more probably it was a case for containing incense. A ram's head upon it would indicate that it belonged to Ramsey Abbey. It is now in the possession of W. Wells, Esq., and Mr. Lawrance has a good photograph of it. Its length is 11 inches. There were also a silver censer and a silver chandelier, on which was a representation of Peterborough Cathedral.

CHAPTER VI.

EARLY CULTIVATION OF THE BED OF THE MERE.
CLAYING AND WARPING.

The whole area had to be prepared by hand. Light harrows were drawn over the land, seed was sown, and again the harrowing was repeated at a cost of 5s. or 6s. an acre. Some parts were dug or forked at 25s. or 30s. per acre. It was three or four years before the cracks disappeared. Cole-seed and ryegrass were the earliest crops taken. At first the latter throve. Then the former produced crops of the value of 30s. per acre. The soil was covered with shells, and being impregnated with animal matter soon became available for wheat. In 1853 the fields were waving with corn where the clay or gault was 15 feet below the surface. Mr. Wells

POST OR GAUGE.

SHOWING THE DEPRESSION OF SOIL SINCE THE DRAINAGE OF WHITTLESEA MERE.

undertook to cover the peat soil with clay, dug at a short distance and transported by means of a temporary tramway. Good crops of corn are now growing on land which was selected in 1851, as being some of the lowest in the neighbourhood, for the purpose of ascertaining by experiment the future subsidence of the soil. It may be stated that the level of the marsh at that time was 9 feet above datum (or the ordinary low-water mark) at Lynn Free-Bridge. The ordinary high-water mark is about 20 feet above the same. An iron post was driven into the underlying bed of gault by a monkey, so that it was fixed firm and immovable. The top of the post is now left on a level with the surface of the soil. A scale of feet and inches had been previously painted on the iron. The part of the post exposed in 1860 was 4 feet 9 inches, showing an average subsidence of 9 inches each year. The bed of the Mere in the same period was lowered 3 feet 6 inches. The gauge in 1875 proved a subsidence of 8 feet 2 inches. The photograph of the harvest-field, in which the gauge stands, affords some idea of the fertility of the soil, and also shows an extraordinary amount of subsidence since the year 1851, when the level of the whole field ranged with the top of the gauge.

As a matter of detail respecting the compression of peat, I may state the result of Mr. Stephen

Ballard's observations while engaged in constructing the Great Northern Railway across Holme Fen. The upper level of the line was raised 4 feet above the surface of the Fen, and the shrinking or compression of the embankment there formed was so great as to render necessary seven times the quantity of material that would have been required for the same construction before the drainage of the Mere. There was the same quantity of peat as at first, but it was in a more solid and compact state in consequence of pressure. Another portion of the peat was found to pass away and evaporate in gases. This waste is going on rapidly in the well-cultivated parts of the Fens, and where there is not much depth of peat the clay will soon approach to the surface of the soil.

The advantage of claying Fen lands was discovered by accident in Colney Fen by one Captain Clay. He emptied a drain, and disposed of its contents by spreading them upon the adjoining black soil. A large increase in the crop of the following year proved the value of the clay. Others followed his example, and it has now become the acknowledged mode of cultivation of the Fens wherever the clay can be found tolerably near the surface. Trenches are cut at intervals, the clay is disinterred and spread over the land, and the black soil is returned to the trench. Claying is not supposed to be remunerative if the clay lies more than 5 feet from the surface. There is much difference in the degrees of fertility caused by the application of different sorts of clay. The best test is to dip a lump of the clay in vinegar, and the more effervescence there is the more profitable it will be in the cultivation of the Fen soil. In the Littleport and Downham district 30,000 acres were drained by two engines; and a machine was invented by Mr. Savage which was intended to turn up the clay like a dredger, but it was not found to answer. In 1860 dry-warping was undertaken in this neighbourhood at a cost of 14*l*. 17*s*. 6*d*. an acre. A coating of 6 inches of clay was fixed for arable land and 4 inches for pasture—all ploughing to be shallow—scarifying and grubbing to a great depth not permitted. All stagnant water was drawn off, and for this purpose drains were cut 2 chains apart. At the last draw, 4 or 5 feet deep, a shoulder or ledge was left on which the last foot of turf rested, like an inverted wedge, leaving a hollow drain underneath to carry off the water.

The details of the expense of dry-warping in 1864 were given to me in conversation with Mr. Hole, superintendent of the works at Holme.

Cost of one acre.

	£	s.	d.
Burning the sedge	0	18	0
Breast ploughing	0	5	0
Levelling and digging the ground	2	10	0
Draining, as described above	0	10	0
Spreading clay, 3½*d.* per yard	7	13	9
Machinery, cost of waggons and plant	12	4	0
Fen tax	0	5	9
Local taxes	0	3	0
Total	24	9	6

The state of cropping of the 3,000 acres, formerly the bed of Whittlesea Mere, in 1860, and the reed shoals:—

	Acres.
Wheat	600
Oats	500
Seeds	150
Cole-seed	150
Mangold	100
Additional wheat	200
Oats	200
Grass	100
Green crops	100
Total	2,100

The present growth [1] per acre is calculated—

	Per acre.
Wheat	5 to 6 quarters.
Oats	7 to 8 ,,
Beans	3 ,,
Mangold	40 tons.
Clover	2 ,,
Potatoes	7 to 8 tons.
Carrots	10 ,,

[1] 'Quarterly Journal of Agriculture,' vol. xxi., p. 135.

VALUE OF CROPS.

According to this calculation, the total value amounts to 12,350*l.*

Wheat is provided for .	. 3,329 persons.
Oats ,,	. 307 horses.
Beef ,,	. 382 persons.
Mutton ,,	. 306 ,,

In 1862 W. Knowles rented 2 acres within 200 yards of Holme village (once snipe-ground), and he grew on those two acres—

	£	s.	d.
Wheat, 7 quarters 6 bushels . . Value	19	6	0
Potatoes, 10 tons . . . ,,	28	3	6
Seed and little ones . . . ,,	1	10	0
Straw 2 loads . . . ,,	5	0	0
Total . .	53	19	6

This holding was shown to the late Mr. Philip Frere, Secretary to the Royal Agricultural Society, and the process was explained by which this extraordinary produce was obtained.

On the same two acres in 1864 he grew—

	£	s.	d.
Wheat, 8 quarters . . . Value	14	0	0
Potatoes, 7¾ tons . . . ,,	27	3	6
Seed . . . . . ,,	1	10	0
Total . .	42	13	6

Mr. John Lawrance told me of the produce in 1864 of 3 acres on a field below Yaxley—on each acre was grown 20 tons of carrots, value 32*l.*

CHAPTER VII.

BREAKING OF MARSHLAND SLUICE.—SIPHONS.

It remains now to notice a temporary failure, in consequence of an inundation, which took place by the side of Marshland Cut in 1862. I was in London when the news arrived that Marshland Sluice was in ruins. It is difficult to conceive the consternation of the Commissioners and the dismay of Mr. Walker, the engineer. The river was guarded by a sluice, which permitted the exit of the upland water as the tide receded, but prevented its entrance when the tide returned. It was constructed soon after 1844, before Whittlesea Mere was drained. The inhabitants of Marshland opposed the passing of the Middle Level Act, and a clergyman is reported to have predicted that 'Whittlesea Mere would come down here.' The tidal water first oozed underneath the cill of the sluice; and, as no effectual means were taken to stop it, its power and volume gradually increased, till at length the whole fabric gave way at once; the salt-water rushed up Marshland Cut, and at some weak portion of the bank it flowed into the adjoining country. At each succeeding tide there was increased pressure and more water

INUNDATION OF 1862.

overflowed, till at last it was declared that 6,000 acres were drowned. A brief description of a scene which I witnessed during this inundation, in June 1862, may be acceptable. I stood on the bank, close by a breach, many yards wide, which admitted a fresh stream of tidal-water at every return of the tide up the cut. A vast extent of water covered the whole surface of the district before us. Nothing was to be seen but water, except that an occasional farmhouse, and willows, a few posts, and the tops of hedges just appeared above what was now a lake. Here and there was a boat going to or returning from an inundated residence to save the wreck of furniture The whole country, being below the datum level, with an ordinary high tide 20 to 22 feet above it, offered a melancholy prospect. Shortly afterwards I attended with a party of Middle Level Commissioners to inspect the ruins of the bridge and the spot where the siphons have since been erected. Sir John Hawkshaw and Mr. Appold were present. The chairman was chosen, and we all sat on an enormous beam, contemplating the terrible race that was running from the sea, and listening to the various suggestions which were made as to the remedies. All were given in perfect confidence that the course of the water might be arrested. One of the most plausible schemes proposed was that of taking a number of old hulks, filling them with stone, and scuttling them in order across the river. Mr. Appold told us a curious fact—that he had once stood under the Britannia Bridge, and with his own Atlantean shoulders had effected a movement and made a sensible deflection in the iron girder of that enormous structure.

Sir John Hawkshaw was consulted, and his plan was adopted. He drove piles in the narrowest part of the channel for the purpose of confining the rush of water to a narrower channel, and to allow the erection of siphons. The dam effectually stopped the flow of the tide, and the upland water during many years passed safely through it. The number of siphons was sixteen. Soon after the ebb of tide began, and there was a difference of 3 inches of level, a small steam-engine on the bank exhausted a portion of air within each siphon. From that time the rush of water began to pour onward to the sea. An Act of Parliament was obtained, without opposition, to adopt the siphons as a temporary measure. It was subsequently found that 4 inches of level were lost to the upper country in times of high flood. In the wet season of 1851 many acres were drowned; and in 1874 an Act was obtained to restore the sluice on a new site, under the advice and control of Sir John Hawkshaw.

CHAPTER VIII.

INUNDATIONS.

As the overflow of water has been at different periods one of the great difficulties of the Fenman, I will endeavour to make a tabular statement of those inundations which have been the most disastrous.

1236. The sea broke in and made great havoc.

1437. 4,400 acres were overflowed in Wisbeach Fen.

1570. In October Marshland was inundated.

1607. Catt's Bank broke. Marshland again inundated.

1723. The inundation water descended the old Bedford River an hour before flood, and ran through the remains of Denver Sluice towards Cambridge between Littleport and Ely, and the Level was drowned to a great depth.

1795. The Haddenham Hills. The country was all bright except here and there a sallow bush or a few reeds, or some small tract of ground that appeared above the water. About Ely most of the market people came from Soham to Ely in boats. Mr. Stafford let his land for 2s., 3s., or 4s. an acre, which usually let for 10s. or 12s. *Armstrong's 'History of Ely.'*

1799, 1805, and 1809. The 100-foot bank broke in each of these years.

1809, January. Breach of bank; water covered 6,000 acres.

1814 and 1815. Burnt and Littleport Fen were drowned. Manea and Welney districts have been inundated three times since 1807.

1823, November. 3,050 acres. The cause of this flood was putting down a dam at Hermitage Bridge, so that the 100-foot might be cleaned out.

1862. The great inundation, for which proceedings were taken against the Middle Level Commissioners.

CHAPTER IX.

THE NORTH LEVEL.

IT is foreign to my purpose to enter into detail respecting drainage in any other parts of the Level, but I will make one or two exceptions. First as regards the North Level, because the great object to which all improvement is now tending—that is, a natural drainage—has there been more nearly attained at the present time.

See 'Journal of the Royal Agricultural Society,' vol. viii., p. 80.

Previous to the improvement of the Nene outfall this level was in a deplorable state. In 1770 a great inundation took place in consequence of a break in the river banks, and the whole level was 7 or 8 feet under water. In 1799 the washes were drowned, and a severe frost succeeded. The water was frozen to the ground, and the ice became 12 or 13 feet thick in some places. This accumulation of the ice was the principal source of the mischief, causing floods when a thaw came. In 1819 Mr. Rennie

THORNEY ABBEY

made a report; but nothing was done until 1827, when the Nene Act was passed.

1831. The North Level drain, extending a distance of 6 miles, was completed. In 1839 I visited Mr. Tycho Wing, at Thorney, and I well remember the circular which he was then engaged in distributing to the tenants for the purpose of persuading them to grow coleseed and other green crops, the success of which cultivation was at that time considered problematical.

The process of *paring* and *burning* was at that time carried on at Thorney universally by means of a French plough—so called, perhaps, because introduced in 1650 by a colony of French refugees. The usual system was to pare and burn for coleseed; take two crops, one of them oats, the other wheat; then lay down for grass three or more years. Claying is now universal. The Thorney district contains 175,888 acres.

The other exception to my purpose is with respect to Holland Fen, in Lincolnshire, eastward of Boston, of which 22,000 acres were drained by the Black Sluice Drainage Act, passed in 1765. The rental before inclosure was 3,000*l.*; directly after the inclosure it was 25,000*l.*

CHAPTER X.

THE NEW DOCK AT LYNN.

IN 1864 I saw the site of the projected dock at Lynn.

The dock was commenced in 1868. The soil of the excavations is used for making a sound foundation for warehouses and railroads, which run round the dock. Two large doors admit vessels. Large blocks of concrete form the foundation wall, which is chiefly composed of shingly gravel from Hunstanton and Portland cement. The blocks weigh 2 tons and upwards, and can be sunk if necessary 70 feet below the surface.

All the shores hereabout were once the purest white sand, but now they are all mud. This deposit of mud is the source of the fertility of the estuary lands. Several acres have been reclaimed. The soil near the causeway has warped up 12 feet. No reclamation ought to be attempted until patches of grass are growing on the surface. Fertility rapidly increases in proportion to the elevation of the warp.

The cause of the fertility of the warp is the good soil that comes down from the upper country. Particles of manure and also numbers of small fish are brought down by the fresh-water, but the fish immediately die when they enter the salt tidal-water.

It is thought worth while to transport boat-loads of cockle-shells to the surface intended to be reclaimed. These shells have a great tendency to accumulate soil at every flux and reflux of the tide.

CHAPTER XI.

AMOUNT OF PARLIAMENTARY TAXES IN THE THREE LEVELS.

I APPEND some statistics from which the reader may form an approximate estimate of the various sums expended in the improvements which have been recently carried out in the three Levels.

Mr. Dowbarn, clerk to the Middle Level Commissioners, furnishes me with the following particulars:—

As regards the Middle Level.

	£
Taxes consolidated under Act of Parliament amounted to	398,000
Exceptional taxes	5,000
Special tax	120,000
Sluice tax	50,000
Total	573,000

The average amount of rental, after all existing Parliamentary taxes are paid, is 30*s.* an acre.

North Level.

The sums raised by Parliamentary taxes in the North Level were—

In 1873	In 1874
£	£
94,200	91,800
32,200	31,700
114,600 *	111,600
4,300 †	4,300
1,400 ‡	1,400
246,700	240,800

Estuary.

	£	s.	d.
Shares and interest paid up, 1874	320,028	6	6
Ouse Outfall and Lynn expenditure	70,961	16	9
Rents, and other sources	29,157	4	4
Total	420,147	7	7

South Level.

South Level proper consists of 600,000 acres out of 120,000. The districts therein have local charges for pumping, &c., but I have no means of ascertaining the various items of taxation.

In addition to those sums which have been raised by Parliamentary taxes, there is also the expenditure which has been undertaken by the owners for the erection of machinery, warping, claying, as well as the cost of adapting the drains and rivers to the circumstances of an improved outfall.

Upon any reasonable estimate that may be as-

---

* With which is connected Nene Outfall.
† Wayland.   ‡ Nene improvement.

sumed as the basis of a calculation of an acreage tax, it will be apparent that an enormous expenditure has been incurred.

CONCLUSION.

I HAVE now arrived at the conclusion of my third division. My expectations are justified, and the case is proved with which I commenced the enquiry. I stated that Fenmen had achieved a great national work and had promoted a true rational progress. A short extract from Lord Russell's 'Essays on the Christian Religion in Western Countries' will show the opinion of a statesman in confirmation of all that I anticipated. Writing in the quiet of his closet, and casting a philosophic view over the course of national improvement in Europe, he says:

'The science of agriculture has made great progress, and the effects of that progress are to be seen in the great increase of food for man and beast, the great increase of tillage, and the improvement of the means of increasing our green crops. For instance, since the time of Charles I. great sums have been applied in the Fen district to the cutting of rivers and making new channels in the

Bedford Level; but it is only of late years that a skilful engineer (Mr. Walker) has transformed a shallow lake into green-fields producing wheat, barley, oats, turnips, and clover. Such is true progress.'

It now only remains to consider whether there are reasonable grounds for supposing that progress may be carried on in an obvious path open to the future, which succeeding generations may pursue, and whether we may predict that what

> 'We have seen our sons may see,'

viz., a marked and visible increase in the wealth, the comfort, and the happiness of the inhabitants of our native country.

PART IV.

CHAPTER I.

FUTURE OF THE FENS.

I HAVE now to enter on a more difficult part of my undertaking, which is to look forward and endeavour to point out the great lines of improvement which are marked out for the future. We have now the recorded opinions of able engineers, in addition to all the experience of the past, by means of which the true principles of drainage have become thoroughly known and established. If lands are to be successfully drained the best possible outfall must be secured for the discharge of the water. Internal works must be constructed of corresponding depths and dimensions, so as to give a complete *natural* drainage (if practicable) and reduce the pumping-power required to a minimum.

In 1858 the North Level was legally separated from the Bedford Level Corporation. By making a new sluice 8 or 9 miles in length, and cutting off a bend in the river, an additional fall of 10 feet was gained and all pumping-power dispensed with. For forty years they have had a natural drainage, the water falling by its own gravitation to the sea. Why should not the South Level do likewise? An Act was passed in 1827, and some part of the Level was benefited; but no great and comprehensive scheme for giving the whole Level a more perfect and effectual drainage has yet been submitted to Parliament. A new outfall much nearer Lynn is required, and the channel for the water must be straightened. There is at present a loss of fall of several feet, and thus it is rendered necessary to keep the waters in the river some feet above the level of the adjoining lands, to the great peril of the country.

'Journal of Royal Agricultural Society,' vol. 8.

A few extracts from the Reports of engineers will enable us to arrive at some definite conclusions on the subject.

Mr. Rendal, in his Report to the Mayor of Lynn, 1840, says: 'The fall from Lynn harbour to the roads out in the Wash is 7 feet 2 inches.'

In a Report made by Professor Gordon we find it stated that 'between Denver Sluice and Lynn Harbour, assuming an average fall in water of 10 inches per mile, there is an absolute fall of ten feet in the distance of 10 miles. At the present time, with the water low, the fall is about 10 feet from Denver Sluice to the end of the Two-mile Cut at low water.'

I add below a tabular account of the comparative heights of the water at Denver Sluice and on the Free Bridge of Lynn during the high flood of October 1875.

The differences of level confirm my previous statements and afford sufficient evidence that the Middle Level Commissioners have, in their schemes of drainage, proceeded in a right direction, and that the cost, though great, has not been incurred in vain.

Table of high and low water on the Lynn Gauge at Denver Sluice and on the Free Bridge at Lynn.

	Low water on the sea side.		Low water on the Fen side at the same time.		High water on the sea side.		High water on the Fen side at the same time.		Low water on Free Bridge Gauge at Lynn.		High water on Free Bridge Gauge at Lynn.	
1875.	ft.	in.	ft.	in.	ft.	in.	ft.	in.	ft.	in.	ft.	in.
Oct. 19	5	0	11	6	18	0	12	3	1	6*	18	0
,, 20	7	6	7	6	16	3	10	6	1	3*	16	6
,, 21	5	3	12	0	14	0	12	8	0	0	13	6
,, 22	7	9	7	9	13	0	11	9	0	6*	12	3
,, 23	8	0	8	0	14	0	11	9	0	6	13	4
,, 24	9	6	9	6	15	3	12	3	0	6	14	3
,, 25	11	0	11	0	16	0	12	6	0	6*	15	2

* Below Datum.

Sir John Hawkshaw's attention was drawn to the banks of the Two-mile Cut below Lynn, which are falling in annually by the action of the tides. His Report states 'that the destructive action that is going on, and the falling in of the foreshores, has not arrived at a stationary point. Under the existing conditions it is not safe to trust to a natural adjustment; it will be necessary, if the tidal flow is to be kept within its present banks, to render the slopes of the channel uniform and to protect them.' It is best now to do this below low water, and make good the injuries of the slopes by depositing stone below low water, and to cover the slopes, to the depth below water to which they are injuriously acted on (which, I fear, extends to the bottom of the cut), with a layer of the same material above low water—slopes trimmed not less than four to one. The slopes above water should be protected by fascine work. Abrasion and washing away of banks and foreshores is going on in the Marsh Cut. No great mischief is done as yet, but the channel will become more and more irregular in form. It would, perhaps, be too hasty to draw important inferences from a few selected passages of Reports, but I would appeal to the local experience of Fenmen whether we are not now in a position to conclude—

1. That a natural drainage is practicable.

2. That the banks of the Two-mile Cut ought to be stoned and its channel extended to the sands beyond.

3. That the river Ouse should be straightened from Denver to Marshland Sluice.

There still remain to be noticed two important points, which follow as matters of detail, but which open out great sources of improvement to the inhabitants of the whole Level. I mean—

1. Storage of water.
2. The best mode of cultivating the Fen soil.

CHAPTER II.

STORAGE OF WATER.

IN whatever direction we look for the further improvement of the Fens, the supply of fresh water will become more and more an object of consideration, as an indispensable necessity for meeting the requirements of modern life and for satisfying the demands of recent legislation. It is a matter of great congratulation that the towns of Wisbeach and Ely have taken the lead in this important question of the day, the storage of water. From information which I have received from Mr. Horsley, manager of the Wisbeach Water Company, I can confidently state that the great work of supplying the town of Wisbeach with water was undertaken by a company, and that the water runs direct from the chalk formation, about 8 miles distant, through an iron pipe, by gravitation, to a small receiving-well, from which it is pumped direct into the main, extending about another 12 miles to Wisbeach. The works were opened in October 1865, and the whole cost was 24,800*l.*

The Company now pay a dividend of 4 per cent. per annum, and hope soon to pay more. This fact is a still greater cause of congratulation, because, if such an enterprise can be made to pay, the noble example will be more generally followed.

I will add a few facts relative to the water-supply at Ely, which were worked out and recently attested by Mr. Marshall as superintendent-registrar at the meeting of the Ely Level Board of Health, which has been in existence twenty-five years.

The Local Board was established in 1850.

The date of the completion of the works is 1855.

The total cost, 16,000*l.*

The population of the town, 8,000.

The debt will be paid off in ten years.

All cess-pools have been abolished.

35 gallons of water per day are allowed to each person.

An unlimited supply of water is offered to the town.

The consequence of this supply of water is especially manifest in the decrease of the annual average of mortality in Ely, comparing the ten years immediately preceding the introduction of the Act with the two complete decades which have elapsed since. These totals were as follow :—

1845	25·60 per 1000.
1841–1851, before the Act,	23·73 ,,
1851–1861 (first decade since)	20·20 ,,
1861–1871 (second ditto)	19·55 ,,

It is most gratifying to find, as a result of twenty-five years' experience, that there has been a permanent reduction in the mortality of the town from no other cause than the removal of nuisances, a copious public water-supply, and a vigilant officer of health.

CHAPTER III.

FUTURE CULTIVATION.

IN any attempt to forecast the results of the cultivation of the Fens we must look to the practice of the best farmers in the more advanced districts, and from the facts there observed we may be aided in drawing a correct inference as to what is likely to happen hereafter. It is now a general practice to remove the soil with a common plough and to use a subsoil plough, which brings up 2 or 3 feet of the subsoil to the surface. Though no uniformity of system can be prescribed, the five-course system of cropping largely prevails :—

1. Mangolds : cole rabbi or coleseed.
2. Oats.
3. Wheat.
4. Seeds.
5. Wheat.

Mr. Rushton's paper read at the Farmers' Club, 1870.

The Fen soils appear to yield larger supplies of ammonia than of the phosphates, and hence more palpable results have followed the application of phosphatic than of ammoniacal manures. Hence we may conclude that this course of management will continue to be adopted, and we may believe that the tendency of our efforts will be in the direction of—

Natural drainage,
Deep tillage,
Universal claying,
General use of superphosphate of lime and the water-drill.

One more reference to future improvement, and I shall conclude. An Act was passed in 1842 for a gigantic and magnificent undertaking called the Victoria Level. Its object is to conduct the rivers Ouse, Nene, Welland, and Witham to a new general outfall in the centre of the present estuary, and by means of embankment to convert the whole bay on each side of the proposed channel into valuable land. It is estimated that 150,000 acres will thus be reclaimed from the sea. Report of Royal Agricultural Society, vol. 8.

CONCLUSION.

I HAVE now gone through my recollections of past times as regards this Fen country. I may have unintentionally made a few inaccurate statements and some mistakes. Those who discover them have my full permission to quote the line of the Roman poet:

Bœotum in crasso jurares aere natum.

Though the Fens are not generally regarded with much favour, or thought a desirable country to live in, I am attached to them from early associations and long residence. The inhabitants of low countries, as a matter of history, have a deep attachment to their own locality. We are informed that William the Third, when, in the height of his prosperity as King of England, he returned to the Hague, felt a heartfelt happiness at the recollection of his native Fen, which the rewards of wealth, power, and ambition were unable to confer. This visit is beautifully described in Macaulay's 'History of England,' vol. iv. p. 2 :

'Thousands had assembled at Houslaerdyk to welcome him with applause, which came from their hearts, and which went to his heart. That was one of the few white days of a life, beneficent indeed and glorious, but far from happy. After more than two years passed in a strange land the exile had again set his foot on his native soil. He heard again the language of his nursery; he saw again the scenery and the architecture which were inseparably associated in his mind with the recollections of childhood and the sacred feeling of home.'

I need not further continue the quotation, but such feelings I am glad to endorse and appropriate. For the Fens and their inhabitants I shall ever feel a deep sympathy and attachment, and it will be a source of future satisfaction to me that I have endeavoured to put together some fragments, however imperfect, which may serve to illustrate and to prove the progress and improvement of the country in which I reside.

APPENDIX

APPENDIX.

ENGLISH FEN AND IRISH BOG.

I HAVE thought it worth while to add an Appendix to my work, with a view to instituting a comparison between English Fen and Irish Bog, principally suggested by a summer excursion in the north of Ireland. I shall show that there are many striking points of similarity between them; that the same prejudice exists against the country and its inhabitants; that the deposits of peat are the same; that many of the fossils and vegetable productions are common to both; that buried timber, antlers of deer, and utensils of wood and iron of the same kind have been at various times disinterred in both.

I shall endeavour to account for the origin and formation of Irish Bog, and with this object in view, I have collected some interesting facts respecting the falling of timber, the storms to which Ireland is periodically liable, and the movement of bogs which occasionally takes place.

I shall proceed to notice the extent of the Irish bogs, and the prospect of making them available for the public good by drainage and the utilization of peat; and I hope that the just inference may be drawn, that sufficient encouragement exists for the owners and occupiers of the peat deposit to persevere in the prosecution of their schemes of improvement, and that they will never rest satisfied till they have made fertile that enormous extent of unproductive soil and rendered it an element of national wealth.

My mode of procedure in this enquiry will be similar to that pursued in my previous chapters; viz., I shall extract largely from authorities which I believe to be trustworthy, and always allow them to tell their own story; except where any observations of my own are necessary to connect the extracts.

Section I.

Character of the Irish Bog Country and its Inhabitants.

ONE of the first points of resemblance between English Fen and Irish Bog is the prejudice which has prevailed against the bog and its inhabitants, climate, and atmosphere, at least in the earlier periods of its history. This prejudice has been already shown to exist in the case of the English Fen; and Mullins in his 'History of Ireland' represents the same feeling in 1724.

He there states that 'the inconveniences of these bogs are very great, a considerable part of the kingdom being rendered useless by them; they keep people at a distance from one another and consequently hinder them in their affairs. These bogs are a great hindrance from place to place; they are a great destruction to cattle; they are a shelter to Tories and thieves. The smell of vapours that arise from bogs is accounted very unwholesome, and the fogs that arise therefrom are commonly putrid, for the rain will not sink into them, there being hardly any substance of its softness more impenetrable to water than turf.'

A question now arises, admitting these facts to be true, how the obloquy is to be averted; and the answer will be that there is sufficient evidence to show that the whole character of the country and its inhabitants can be completely changed by the exertions of well-directed industry, skill, and capital, and be thereby elevated to a high state of culture and civilization.

Section II.

Buried Remains and Fossils.

THERE is also a similarity between the Fen and the Bog, in that the same sort of buried remains, fossils, and utensils of wood and iron are common to both. But a peculiarity exists in the Irish peat-mosses which is worthy of notice, viz., the high state of preservation of animal substances buried in them for long periods. In Lyell's 'Principles of Geology' (chap. 44) it is stated that 'on the estate of the Earl of Moira in the north of Ireland a human body was dug up in gravel covered with eleven feet of peat. The body was completely clothed and the garments seemed to be made of hair. Before the use of wool the clothes of the inhabitants were made of hair, so that it would appear that the body had been buried at that early period; yet it was fresh and unimpaired.' This account is confirmed by an extract from an old book entitled Mullins's 'History of Ireland,' printed at Dublin by George Grierson in 1766, and containing a collection of papers communicated to the Royal Dublin Society referring to some curiosities in Ireland. It is there stated: 'I know not if it be worth observing that a turf-bog

Mullins, p. 137.

preserves things strangely. A corpse will lie entire in one for several years. I have seen a piece of leather pretty fresh dug out of a turf-bog, that had never in the memory of man been dug out before. Butter has been found that had lain above twenty years, and, though not fit to be eaten, served to grease wood. Trees are found sound and entire in them, and those birch and alders which are very subject to rot. The trees are supposed by the vulgar to have lain there ever since the Flood; but the truth is they fell on the surface of the earth, and the bog swelling by degrees at last covered them, and, being of an oily vegetable substance, it like a balsam preserves them. The trees burn very well, and serve for torches. I have seen them used as lights for catching of salmon.'

With reference to the fossil remains of the Elk, there is an interesting discourse on the subject of long horns found underground in Ireland by Thomas Molyneux, Fellow of Queen's College, Dublin. The opinion maintained by him is that the antlers were not those of the elk, but of the moose deer. Mr. Henry Osborn, resident in the county of Meath, near Drogheda, sent the following account of the manner and place in which they were found :—

'I have, by bearer, sent the head and horns. This is the third head I have found by casual trenching in my orchard. They were all dug up within the compass of an acre of land, and lay about four or five feet in a boggy soil. The first pitch was of earth, the next two or three feet of turf, and then followed a sort of white marl, where they were found. To them I could add other substances of the like. To my own knowledge twenty or thirty pairs of these horns have been dug up in several parts of the country. These may be sufficient to show that this creature was formerly common with us in Ireland. I known they are called by ignorant people, nay, and some of the learned vulgar in the country, Elches horns. This is an error, the elks are too small to support such large branching horns as are found. We must look out and try if we can discover some other quadruped, whose size and description will better agree with our Irish animal than that of the Elche does; and after all our enquiries we shall not discover any one that in all respects exactly answers it, save only that lofty-horned animal in the West Indies called a "Mousse."'

Mr. Arthur Young, in his 'Irish Tour,' states that there are 'evident marks of the plough fourteen feet below the surface of the peat soil, also remains of cabins, cribs for cattle, Moose's horns, oaks, yews, fir, being good red deal.'

Mr. R. L. Edgeworth found at the bottom of his moss, fifteen feet deep, a turner's shop, arrows, bowls, and other wooden utensils. *Archæologia, vol. vii.*

The following is a statement made to me by Mr. Burgess, of Parkanaur, Dungannon, relative to the deposits in peat bog:—

' I have remarked in my own bogs the layers of different species of trees, as if left there by repeated revolutions in the natural world. The first or lowest layer was yew mixed with hazel and the shells of nuts. The second layer was oak, black and solid. The last, which appears to be the latest tree of the ancient days, was pine-fir, of the Scotch tribe seemingly—we call it Bogwood. From its resinous quality it ignites instantaneously and creates a blazing fire, and astonishes those who are strangers to our country. The decomposed vegetable matter, consisting of leaves and plants, is that which is cut for turf and used for fuel. It grows, and if not cut will form a stratum of many feet. This has been proved, by various articles having been dropped ages ago on an early surface. I have heard of an old knife; I have seen myself a hat—the same as worn in the time of Elizabeth. The trees found are frequently charred.' In Percy's 'Metallurgy,' in the chapter on Peat, we find that 'in some cases forests have grown over peat-bogs; in others peat has accumulated in forests and finally destroyed them. Thus fir-trees occurring in Irish bogs have generally six or seven feet of compact earth underneath their roots, and they are found standing as they grow. In the case of oak, their roots are commonly found resting on the gravel at the base and on the sides of small hillocks of sand.'

Section III.

Origin and Formation of Irish Bog.

Ellis, chap. iii. p. 97.

THE surface of Irish bog has never been disturbed by inundations from the sea, and consequently there are no marine deposits. The peat and moss are generally supposed to have been formed by the destruction of growing timber by the removal of soil, in consequence of the terrific storms to which Ireland has ever been periodically liable, as well as by a multiplicity of streams and an exuberant vegetation, among which the *Sphagnum palustre* is conspicuous—a plant having the property of throwing new shoots from its upper part while its lower extremities are decaying. In order to exemplify the manner in which chemical action operates upon timber when destroyed, and how the wood or fibre is converted into peat, I have made an extract from the 'Chemistry of Creation,' by Robert Ellis, F.L.S.

'In examining the chemical history of this substance it may be profitable to select an anecdote of forest life in regions where sun and air and rain, together with other co-operating causes, act more powerfully than in our temperate climate. The inhabitants of the vast primæval forests of the New World are frequently startled by the crash of falling timber, which, after centuries of increasing strength and grandeur, has at length fallen a victim to the exhaustive influences of time and old age. No sooner has it fallen than a number of agents set to work to effect its complete destruction. The rain-drops from heaven saturate it, the burning solar ray darts down upon it, and, favoured by the temperature, the air begins to act chemically on the prostrate trunk. Insects come and bore long galleries through its sides; ants and beetles also drill their holes through and through, and others eat away its bark. The rain and air get access to the very heart of the tree. By and by all the insects have taken their departure. The sun, wind, and rain have been nevertheless incessantly acting upon it. And now a tribe of painted fungi, of the most curious forms and colours, sit upon the crumbling mass. Another portion of time glides away. Where is the prostrate tree? The place which for centuries it covered with the grateful shade of its broad branches has forgotten even its existence. "The place thereof knoweth it no more." Is it so? Is the tree not there? Surely it is; but its elements have all long since passed into another form. The tree has crumbled into dust, and the dust has blended with the earth and can no longer be distinguished therefrom. How has this great change been effected? By what means has the hard and unyielding woody fibre of this giant tree been broken up and left a mass of powder? Chemistry gives the reply, and informs us that it is by successive chemical decomposition that the loftiest inhabitant of the woods has fallen and entered into the common home of all living things, where the great and the small, even among plants, rest together. When woody fibre is moistened and freely exposed to the action of the atmosphere it immediately begins to undergo chemical decomposition. There is an interchange of ingredients between it and the air. There is also a certain quantity of heat evolved. The fibre alters its external characters, changes colour, and loses tenacity. In common language, it is said to be rotting. This process goes on, the colour deepens until at length it becomes brown, and the mass is so friable as to crumble to pieces in the hand. This is vegetable mould, strictly so called, chemically produced. It must, therefore, be regarded as a layer of material in which continual processes of decomposition are going forward. Vegetable mould in this condition is called " humus." When decay has proceeded to a certain length the constituents have become so entirely altered and reconstructed that this decomposition no longer takes place. In this condition mould is analogous to peat, which may be defined to be vegetable fibre which has undergone comparatively complete decay.'

Having shown the way in which chemical action may operate on timber which has fallen and decayed, it may be interesting to have an account of the forces which act upon the growing trees and occasion their overthrow and destruction.

Mr. Burgess gave me an extract from his private journal, dated January 1, 1839, which illustrates the violence of the storms in Ireland and their possible effects on the formation of bogs.

'*January* 1.—We went to Oriel Temple, the residence of Lord Ferrard. At this time it was at its highest beauty, but it was of short duration. On Sunday night a storm left it in a few hours in a complete state of desolation. I shall never forget the roaring of the winds on that awful night. The house was actually shaking, the portraits flapping on the walls. On a sudden there was a most dreadful crash, caused by an immense tree falling on the portico outside. Soon after, another crash and another. The winds continued howling until daybreak; when, on looking out, I perceived the fine dark wood of silver fir, which sheltered one of the ponds in front of the house, cut in two, and showing the appearance of a broken-masted fleet. The grounds around the Temple were covered with prostrate trees. As the morning light increased, more desolation appeared. We first tried to make our way to the American grounds, which we left in the morning in all their winter beauty. Here a scene of desolation met our eyes. The wonderful specimens of various trees from every clime, collected by the late Lord Oriel, were lying in a confused mass together. The gorgeous pines and *abies*, the unique lyon cedars, and various specimens of cypress lay, never to rise again. From thence we walked to the lake. Here was the same scene of havoc: one oak lying over another and the drive quite covered with trunks and branches. The winds were still howling. The clouds, one darker than another, passing in wild confusion, with now and then a gleam of light. Well I remember that lurid combination of forms awful and terrible above, and the ruinous devastation below. This quick and sudden transition from everything that was beautiful to perfect desolation very much impressed my mind that the bogs of Ireland had been in time past formed by similar natural causes.'

Mullins, in his 'History of Ireland,' describes a flood in

1706, which 'carried away several bridges and the sides of a mountain, laying abundance of houses two or three feet under water; and in 1707, in the county of Antrim, there was a similar flood which devastated the country, tearing up large rocks and leaving meadows two or three feet deep with sand.'

Having thus described the circumstances of the probable origin of peat, I will endeavour to follow the subsequent history of this wonderful stratum.

Section IV.

Moving Bogs.

LYELL, in his 'Principles of Geology,' (chap. xliv., p. 510,) states that in Ireland bogs have burst and sent forth volumes of black mud, which has been known to creep over the country at the rate of ordinary currents, and sometimes to overwhelm woods and cottages and leave a deposit of bog and peat fifteen feet thick.

I shall now give an extract relative to the moving bog of Kilmaleady, in King's County,[1] from a paper written by Richard Griffith, mining engineer:—

Dublin Society Journal, vol. i. xviii.

'The bog of Kilmaleady, from whence the eruption took place, is near the village of Clara, in King's County. It contains 500 acres, in many places forty feet deep, bounded on all sides, except the south, by steep ridges of highland composed of limestone rock and containing subterranean streams. The southern face of the bog is open

[1] It began June 26, 1821, and 150 acres of cornfields and pastures were covered with peat moss.—'Steele on Peat Mosses,' p. 300.

to a moory valley, through which a stream runs 18 feet wide. This bog, like all other deep and wet bogs, is composed for the first 8 or 10 feet of a reddish-brown spongy mass formed of still undecomposed fibres of bog moss (*Sphagnum palustre*), which, by capillary attraction, absorbs water in great quantities. Beneath this fibrous mass the bog gradually becomes pulpy, till at length, towards the bottom, it assumes the consistence of black mud heavier than water. The surface of the bog is 20 feet above the level of the valley, from which it rose at a steep angle. Owing to the dryness of the season the inhabitants were enabled to sink turf-holes 10 feet below the surface of the valley—in fact, until they reached the blue clay which forms the substratum of the bog. The lower, or pulpy, muddy part gave way and floated the upper part of the bog, which continued to move with astonishing velocity along the valley to the southward, forcing before it not only clumps of turf on the edge of the bog but even patches of moory meadows to the depth of several feet, the grassy surface of which heaved and turned over like the waves of the ocean, and very soon the whole valley, to the breadth of a quarter of a mile, was covered to the depth of 8 to 10 feet. Two hilly barriers retarded and altered its course. It was at last stopped by drawing off water and opening the course of the stream. The head of water was lowered and the bog ceased to flow. The whole distance through which the bog had flowed is about 3 miles in length.'

By the eruption of the peat-bog of Poulenard, in the county of Louth, which happened in December 1793, the ground was covered in many places 20 feet deep, and many houses and bridges were destroyed. A part of the Moss of Kincardine, in Perthshire, has frequently been inundated by water, which carried an immense volume upon the ad- (Philosophical Transactions, vol. xxii.)

jacent village and arable lands, where it overwhelmed everything that stood in its way. A similar overflowing of the Moss of Solway, in Dumfries-shire, took place in November 1771. It was carried down a narrow glen, between two banks 300 feet high, into a spacious plain, which it overspread. By this means, 800 acres of fine arable land were covered with moss soil from 3 to 15 feet deep, and the houses of 27 families were destroyed.

Section V.

Extent of Irish Bog. Prospects of Drainage and Reclamation.

HAVING endeavoured in some measure to explain the way in which peat-mosses have accumulated, and how their contents have been poured over adjoining districts, I shall now briefly state the extent of the bogs and the success which may be expected to ensue from the processes of drainage and reclamation.

In a Report of the Commissioner appointed to inquire into the nature and extent of bogs in Ireland, and the practicability of draining and cultivating them, printed for the House of Commons, April 28, 1814, we find a statement 'that, from data on which reliance can be placed, the extent of peat soil exceeds 2,800,000 English acres, large proportions of which might be converted to the general purposes of agriculture.' The Report further states that the fair average of engineering report is: 'From an expenditure of 1*l.* to 20*l.* the reclamation would recover a permanent interest of 15*l.* to 20*l.* on the expenditure.'

In a volume entitled 'Metallurgy,' by John Percy, F.R.S. (chapter on Fuel, p. 202), it is stated that 'in Ireland, of which the total area is 20,000,000 acres, it was estimated in 1845 that the total area of bog was 2,830,000 acres, or nearly one-seventh of the entire surface of the island; 1,575,000 acres of which is called flat bog, 1,254,000 acres of mountain bog. The flat bog is spread over the central portion of the great limestone plain; the mountain bog is chiefly distributed through the hilly country along the coast. The central district deserves most attention.'

Among the Reports made during the Vienna Universal Exhibition of 1873 there is an article by Mr. Paget which deserves attention. He observes: *Part ii. p. 334.*

'It is, perhaps, not generally known or remembered that the Dutch, during the reign of William III. and Mary, offered to drain and reclaim into pasture the whole of the great Irish bog of Allan, in Queen's County, if only allowed to be governed by their own laws. As their bog is lying waste to this day, and as an important example has been lost, many will regret that the offer was not accepted. Perhaps it is not even now too late. Some of the richest soils in Ireland are, however, said to be due to a mode of cultivation very similar to the Dutch plans introduced by emigrants popularly known in Ireland by the name of Palatins, and possibly of German and Dutch descent.'

I have not been able to procure much information on the progress of recent reclamation, but I think we may infer, from the foregoing references, that the extent of bog has not been materially diminished in late years. Opinions, however, still differ as to whether the drainage of extensive bogs is practicable, and also whether the outlay would prove a profitable investment. As the result of private enquiry, I subjoin two statements. One is the manager's report of the cultivation of the bogs of Parkanaur, which have been converted into valuable land: 'The turf to be removed; 1 to 3 feet of peat left. If the fall is sufficient, a drain was cut in the clay soil below the peat; clay laid in the autumn to be pulverised by frost. In spring a dressing of lime is laid on; a course then, in successive years, of potatoes, turnips, or mangolds, rye with seeds. Another dressing of clay, and afterwards an alternate system of green cropping succeeded by grain.'

In six or seven years the outlay will be amply repaid by a rent from 30s. to 3l. the English acre.

I have another report, from a reliable source, stating:

'I do not believe it possible to reclaim deep bog profitably. It takes three years' cutting down, 3 or 4 feet deep each year; and you cannot cut deeper, or the soil will fall in.

'In wet bogs you cannot drain more than 2 feet each year, and I believe that the drainage of large wet regular bogs does not pay.'

Section VI.

Utilization of Peat.

This is a subject still to be noticed, which is of great national importance, and to which public attention has lately been turned. It was stated in the Report of the Vienna Exhibition, 1873, that in Holland not less than 40,000,000 tons of peat fuel are raised and dried each year, yielding an excise duty of 140,000l. per annum.

January, 1869.

In the fifth volume of the 'Dublin Society's Journal' we find an interesting paper describing the process by which Robert M. Alloway made the use of peat profitable.

It is there stated that 'Providence did not intend so singular and coal-like a substance should always lie waste, but that it was capable of being made profitable.' A manufactory was set up in Queen's County twenty years ago. It was thought that by artificial condensation peat might be made more profitable and valuable as fuel. Compression and artificial desiccation were tried. Among the most noteworthy of those who turned their attention to this subject was Lord Willoughby d'Eresby. But the machinery was too expensive, and the several factories were closed.

The method of Mr. Alloway comprised two processes; he enlisted in his service the sun in summer and rain in winter. The first process was breaking up the raw material and disintegrating the peat. The second process was moulding the peat into 'pats,' which were placed in store-houses from April to November. It could be made and dried in less than a week. It was then condensed. The advantage of this method of manufacture was that the peat was quite free from noxious gases. Peat is good fuel for generating steam. From 10,000 tables, 50,000 tons could be turned out in six months, price 10*s.* per ton.

In the 'Journal of the Royal Dublin Society,' 1872, Professor Reynolds has recorded his opinion that the peat-fields of Ireland can be made available for industrial purposes; and Mr. Siemens, in the same Journal, has stated that, after a certain process in a gas-furnace, peat has the preference over Staffordshire coal in working furnaces. It is also stated in 'Steele on Peat-mosses' 'that in Kincardine and Blair Drummond, in Perthshire, peat-mosses have been rendered productive and populous.'

I have lately had some communication with Mr. Sydney B. J. Skertchly, of H.M. Geological Survey, who has been engaged for four years in making the Geological Survey of the Fens. He has kindly addressed a letter to me; and I insert it as a fitting conclusion and an interesting practical comment upon the information I have endeavoured to collect from various sources on the subject of Fens.

'H.M. Geological Survey, Brandon:
'Nov. 9, 1875.

'Dear Sir,—I have read with interest your chapter on the Fenland deposits, and beg leave to send you a few notes thereon.

'*Peat.*—It is not at all necessary to suppose that peat is formed in consequence of the obstruction to the flow of water by the destruction of forests; because (1) peat often grows where there are no buried trees, (2) peat often underlies the trees, and must, therefore, have commenced forming before they began to grow, (3) so far as I know, the buried forests are always confined to the vicinity of the highland: this is certainly the case in this district and in Ireland. Peat, in fact, began to form when a damp climate favoured the luxuriant growth of moss. There were intervals of comparative dryness, during which it ceased to be produced; and during them the trees crept over the peat surface from the bordering forests. When the requisite climatal conditions again obtained, peat again commenced to grow, and began to bury the trunks of the *living* trees, whose death was caused partly by the exclusion of air from their roots, (for this will kill trees, as was found in the case of some fine elms in Hyde Park, round whose trunks a quantity of soil was banked), and partly by chilling the trunk and preventing the circulation of the sap. The trees thus killed begin to rot at the place to which the peat reaches, and finally the dead trunks succumb to the prevalent winds.

Violent storms are not necessary to ensure their fall, though they, of course, exert their powers in that direction; and the fact that most of the buried trees in the Fen lie with their heads to the north-east shows that the south-west wind laid them low, and proves that in those far-off times that wind, as now, was the prevalent one. I may add, that there are several distinct horizons of buried forests in the Fens, which will be described in detail in my forthcoming Memoir on the Geology of the Fenland.

'*Shells in the Gravel.*—I believe there are records of two faunas preserved in the Fen gravels, a hot and a cold one; though we cannot separate the deposits belonging to each, from their being much mixed together. The former is characterised by the presence of the lion, elephant, &c., and such shells as *Cyrena fluminalis*—a modern Nile species—and the latter by the woolly rhinoceros, mammoth, &c., and such shells as *Astarte* and *Cyprina Islandica*. The *Tellina solidula* you quote as an Arctic form is, I fear, a mistake; for, although it does live in Arctic seas, it is found as far south as Madeira.

'*Fauna.*—To the animals you cite may be added the bison, wolf, bear, and pelican, as interesting examples of the old Fen fauna; also the remains of man in the bronze and stone celts, hatchets, arrows, sling-stones, scrapers, &c., which have been abundantly exhumed from the Fens.

'Yours very truly,

'SYDNEY B. J. SKERTCHLY.'

'J. M. Heathcote, Esq.'

I will now conclude by stating that I have placed this imperfect sketch of the past condition and future prospect of Irish Bog in contrast to my own reminiscences of English Fen, because it gives me an opportunity of expressing my sincere interest in all Low Countries and an earnest hope that all owners and occupiers of Irish Bog will assist in making a national effort to develop the resources of the various bogs which now remain unreclaimed in Ireland and which still disfigure the surface of that beautiful country.